P

MW01006077

WHEN CHURCH IS HARD

Dr. Tyler Johnson's diagnosis of the factors and circumstances catalyzing Latter-day Saint faith crisis in the twenty-first century is spot-on. This book is valuable for both young people trying to figure out whether a Latter-day Saint life is worth the effort and members of older generations trying to understand the world in which their children, grandchildren, and great-grandchildren live. Johnson makes a powerful argument for participation in Church communities as a tool for moral and spiritual formation and as an antidote to the atomization of twenty-first century life.

—MELISSA WEI-TSING INOUYE, author of *Crossings: a bald
Latter-day Saint woman scholar's ventures through life, death,
cancer, and motherhood (not necessarily in that order)* and
Sacred Struggle: Seeking Christ on the Path of Most Resistance

With a deep sense of empathy derived from countless hours of listening to the faith-filled questions, concerns, and doubts of the rising generation, Tyler Johnson offers a lens into why church may be hard for some and how we can make it a welcoming place for all. The invitation here is to seek Jesus and build Zion, an expansive endeavor in Johnson's mind, one in which believers of all stripes find peace and a place to belong.

—W. PAUL REEVE, author of *Let's Talk about Race and Priesthood*

As a physician, Tyler Johnson has dedicated his life to caring for and healing people's physical bodies. In this book, he dedicates himself as a covenanted Latter-day Christian to caring for and healing the body of the Church. He is the doctor we all hope for—the kind that listens deeply, delivers the hard news straightforwardly, and speaks with empathy, compassion, and hard-won experience and expertise. Some of the things Johnson discusses are challenging to read, because as a people we're not used to talking publicly about hard things. But there is presently too much pain in our collective body, and we need to muster all our resources to not only survive but thrive in challenging times. More than being mere food for thought, this is a book that can bring healing across the many divides we see in the Church today.

—PATRICK MASON, author of *Planted: Belief and Belonging in an Age of Doubt*

If you feel like church is hard, this book is for you. If you love anyone who feels like church is hard, this book is for you. Tyler's frank acknowledgment that church can be hard—that my worries are not made up—has helped me feel understood and welcome in ways I didn't before. This book discusses the Church's relationships with race, gender, sexuality, and more with consistent candor and empathy. By offering ways to find meaning and joy in the Church without dismissing my worries, Tyler shows that the Church does in fact have resources for people like me. Because I trust that Tyler truly understands the depth of my concerns, I trust his responses.

—ELIZA WELLS, former Stanford YSA member; PhD candidate, MIT

WHEN CHURCH IS HARD

WHEN CHURCH IS HARD

TYLER JOHNSON

DESERET
BOOK

SALT LAKE CITY, UTAH

Deseret Book is a registered trademark of Deseret Book Company.

Visit us at deseretbook.com

Library of Congress Cataloging-in-Publication Data
(CIP data on file)
ISBN 978-1-63993-182-8

Printed in the United States of America
Lake Book Manufacturing, LLC, Melrose Park, IL

10 9 8 7 6 5 4 3 2 1

*I dedicate this book to Church members who
find themselves on the margins—
and to those who seek to make the Church
a kingdom where everyone belongs.*

*May we all work together
to hasten that day.*

CONTENTS

INTRODUCTION

My patient is a forty-six-year-old woman who was diagnosed with colon cancer two years ago. After an initial surgery to remove the primary tumor, she had received six months of chemotherapy and then begun what we call "surveillance," a nerve-racking period where we hope the cancer will not return but take extensive measures to monitor for its reappearance.

But today, my patient is coming to see me in clinic. I have already reviewed her CT scan and know that it contains the kind of information no patient wants to receive. Sitting across from her in my office, I look her in the eyes and say, as evenly as I can: "Mrs. Smith, I wish I had a different message to bring to you today, but I'm afraid your CT scan indicates that the colon cancer has likely returned. It appears to have spread to the lining of your abdomen. We will need to pursue a biopsy to ensure the imaging means what we think it means, but I want to be candid with you up front about my concerns."

Tears fill her eyes and run down the cheeks of her husband,

seated by her side. We all sit together in the weighty silence settles in the moments after I articulate this difficult news.

In my nearly fifteen years as an oncologist, I've had conversations like this many, many times. Sometimes I have them in the hospital, and sometimes in the cancer center. Regardless of our surroundings, the gravity persists. Speaking to my patients about difficult news remains one of the most solemn—and sacred—parts of my job.

So why do I bring up this story at the beginning of a book about how church can be hard?

Because just a mile from our medical campus sits the chapel where I have served as bishop, bishop's counselor, and institute teacher. The bishop's office there is not unlike a doctor's office—both are nondescript rooms where people go to seek healing. I've spent innumerable hours in that office (as well as strolling around the campus just outside it) talking with young Church-member friends. We rarely talk about cancer, but the conversations can be every bit as hard.

Young people have come there to discuss the place of gay people in the Church, the experience of being a woman in the Church, the Church's history with respect to race, difficult questions in Church history, concerns about the Church's financial dealings, God's apparent silence when the divine presence is desperately needed, and on and on and on.

In the hours I've spent in these discussions, multiple things have become clear: first, a great deal of pain broods over young Church members. Not all young members feel these existential concerns so acutely, but many, many do. Second, young Church members, almost without exception, want *desperately* to do what's right. Their deep-seated concerns about the Church and their place in it nearly always arise precisely because of that bone-deep desire.

2

And, third: this is a matter they treat with enormous seriousness, wanting very much to find truth and live it.

Both as a doctor and as a Church member, I have learned a vital lesson that applies in both spheres—and pretty much everywhere in life. Even though I've spent thousands of hours caring for the sick and dying, and even though I see patients with cancer every week, and even though I've taken my patients through every detail of their MRIs and CT scans, and even though I've spent many hours trying to walk in my patients' shoes—even with all of this, I recognize this fundamental fact:

I do not know what it is like to have cancer.

Similarly, despite all the time and love and energy I've spent with young Church members—especially with those who feel excluded, marginalized, or alone within the Church—this fundamental fact remains true:

I do not know what it is like to be any of them.

I can imagine—and I try to do just that—but it just isn't the same. I can describe the attendant emotions from the outside, but I do not know them viscerally. I can worry and pray and hope on behalf of my patients and my young Church friends, but none of this amounts to the same thing as being inside of their skin.

In this sense, I want to make an important observation. When we talk about "the Church," we may refer to one of two things. Sometimes, "the Church" refers to an institution, a conceptual framework defined by certain theological principles and a certain ecclesiastical structure.

But that's only part of what most of us are talking about when we refer to "the Church."

Most of the time, when a person hears "the Church," what instead comes to mind includes, yes, those abstract principles, but also a particular set of experiences, relationships, and personal beliefs that combine together to define what *that person* understands to be "the Church." I point out this difference because I want those who read this book to know: I have a pretty good sense of what the institutional Church looks like, and I know really well the personal set of experiences, relationships, and beliefs that *I* know as "the Church," but there is no way I can similarly know the experiences, relationships, and beliefs that make up what *you* understand to be "the Church." So, if I say something and it rings hollow or untrue to you—if you think, *That's not the Church I know*—well, this may be the chief reason.

I listen, I imagine, I try—but I ultimately cannot *know* what it is like to be in anyone else's shoes.

And so, this book really contains two different strains of thought. On the one hand, you will hear many stories that reflect, either directly or in abstract/composite form, the stories I've heard from those who've counseled with me over the years. On the other, you will hear my own yearnings and spiritual wanderings, the way I have processed the scriptures and other books, the ways in which I have sometimes become sad or angry, frustrated or impatient, confused or forlorn, yet also joyful and filled with meaning, at peace and full of beauty—and the way in which I've ultimately tried to draw all of this together into a meaningful whole. None of that means that I am "right," and I don't pretend that anything here is definitive or official—but this is my sincere attempt to find order, beauty, and meaning in a world that is often chaotic and confusing.

I hope that my reflecting on the stories of others will still hold great meaning. Even though I can ultimately really understand life only in my own skin, there is yet something to be said for *accompanying* those who suffer. Accompanying is not the same as suffering, but it still affords a unique and sacred understanding that can come only from suffering closely observed. If nothing else, I can say this: I have listened, and listened, and listened some more.

And as I've listened, I've felt my heart begin to change.

I am a different person because of the stories I've heard and the suffering I've seen up close.

And that is largely the genesis for this book.

In that vein, I want to say something out loud right here up front: I know that Church membership can involve real pain, and I acknowledge that my life in the Church has been easier than that of many others. Because my overlapping identities fit me into a relatively comfortable place in the gospel family, I've never felt the personal sting of rejection or exclusion within the Church; it would be condescending to pretend to know what that sting is really like. I *know* that I don't know.

So why then would I write this book? Perhaps a brief story will illustrate the impulse that drove the writing. When I was about sixteen, I encountered my first bout of what I would now call existential angst. One night, I said to my dad that I felt like I didn't fit in. But I didn't simply mean that I wasn't particularly popular (though that was true, too), but rather that I wondered about my place in the universe—what could a little nothing like me mean amidst the wheeling galaxies and a universe filled with smoldering, burnt-out stars? I might have been channeling Whitman (though I couldn't have quoted him back then), who wrote:

> *Oh me! Oh life! Of the questions of these recurring,*
> *Of the endless trains of the faithless, of the cities filled with*
> *   the foolish, [. . .]*
> *Of the poor results of all, of the plodding and sordid crowds*
> *   I see around me,*
> *Of the empty and useless years of the rest, with the rest of me*
> *   intertwined,*

*The question, oh me! So sad, recurring—What good amid
these, oh me, oh life?*

Of course, Whitman offers his own answer ("The powerful
play goes on and you may contribute a verse"). But that evening
in our little home, my dad didn't quote from Whitman, but rather
from Eliza R Snow. Taking a hymnal down off the bookshelf, my
dad read me this:

> *For a wise and glorious purpose*
> *Thou hast placed me here on Earth.*
> *But withheld the recollection*
> *Of my former friends and birth.*
> *Yet oft'times, a secret something*
> *Whispered: "you're a stranger here."*
> *And I felt that I had wandered*
> *from a more exalted sphere.*[1]

I cannot explain what happened when I read that text that
night. It was not just that it sounded nice or that it comforted
me or even that it suggested a powerful idea. Rather, the force of
the theological concepts Eliza Snow conveys in those brief verses—
premortal existence, the eternity of the soul, the existence of loving
heavenly parents, the presence of a veil, the purpose of earthly existence, the possibility of returning to our heavenly home, and on
and on—was a balm to the wound in my soul. The text dissolved
what moments before had seemed insoluble granite. These ideas—
this doctrine—spoke to my deepest aching need.

And that's a big part of the reason I wrote this book. There is
often pain and discomfort that comes with modern Church membership, but I believe we must face these problems squarely because
beyond them lies a theology with great power to heal a wounded

world. The gospel sings sweet songs to comfort the ailing and aimless among us.

This book reflects merely one person's take on these complex and nuanced questions. I pray I've listened closely enough to those who are teaching me that I will have something meaningful to say in response. More than anything, whatever I may get right or wrong, I hope this book will bring healing.

After all, I'm a doctor: that's what I try to do.

And on that note, let me say one thing more, and to a different group of people. Presumably, a lot of people who read this will be those for whom church is hard. But if you are buying the book for someone like that while feeling secure in your own testimony, may I invite you to read the book too? Because, as important as it is for those who are suffering to know they are heard, let me say this plainly: it is perhaps even more vital that those who are not currently suffering *better understand the source of that overwhelming pain.* In part, this understanding is needed because it will build a bridge over what often feels like a growing intergenerational divide. But, beyond that, that kind of understanding matters because with it we keep our covenant to mourn with those who mourn. And, finally, as someone who was *more comfortable* before my hundreds of hours of listening, I will say this: I needed the listening because it broke open my heart and taught me just a bit about how to be more like Jesus.

So, in this book, I do not promise easy answers. Indeed, for some, I imagine this book will complicate—not simplify—their discipleship. I do not offer easy answers because I do not believe the gospel trades in that kind of simplistic resolution. The hope Jesus brings is a hope forever tempered by the suffering of the cross and Gethsemane, and so the answers we find in the gospel most often come as paradoxes: the living among the dead, sacrificing and being blessed tenfold, the penniless being richer than the wealthy, and an immigrant single mother preparing to give birth to God's own son.

No, we will not speak here of easy answers but instead, figuratively, of water flowing from rocks and manna appearing in the desert. Therefore, if you are a person who has always found the gospel to be easy and intuitive, I hope this book will fix your gaze upon the plight of those desperately wanting to do what's right who struggle to know whether a life in the restored Church is the best way to do good in the world. In coming to this understanding, I hope this book will make the gospel harder, but also thereby more fully true.

And if you are one who has all but lost hope that the gospel has meaningful succor to offer, I hope this book will kindle whatever embers still glow in your growing darkness. I am not seeking to convince, but to explore. I hope you will find in these pages a friend you sense has accompanied someone rather like you along what I know can be a hard and lonely road. That these words will bring a measure of healing, and of hope, remains my prayer.

PART 1

WHEN FAITH FALTERS

1

OUR BRAVE NEW WORLD

Questions

- Why is it so hard for me to talk to my parents or other older loved ones about the deep questions and concerns I have about the gospel?
- I get a sense staying in the Church is harder now than it was fifty years ago—why would that be the case?

We all tend to think of ourselves as individuals living our own lives, defined by our immediate surroundings and the relationships that link us to those around us, and to some degree that's true. What we may not recognize immediately (or ever), however, is that cultural forces shape us as well. As one quick example: many people of my generation grew up knowing older people who had lived through the Great Depression. These people are often thrifty to the point of excess and find themselves haunted by the sense that another period of scarcity lurks just around the next corner. This behavior is no accident—it reflects the poverty these people knew as children. That scarcity imprinted on their brains a certain way of seeing the world, and that viewpoint directed their behavior for years afterward.

In ways that are less obvious but no less important, the culture in which we come of age influences and shapes us just as surely as it did them. So, when we consider how we think about the Church, it's helpful for us to recognize context and to think about how it might frame our religiosity. In this chapter, I'll outline four characteristics of our age that will likely sound familiar, in the hopes of allowing you to think about what these may mean for you as you approach your relationship with the Church.

WE ARE BECOMING CYBORGS

Ample survey data from the past twenty years demonstrate that religion is losing its preeminent place as an organizing social structure in the Western world. Data from Pew and other similar surveys demonstrate both that the importance of religion in general is waning and that The Church of Jesus Christ of Latter-day Saints, specifically, is no longer holding sway over its members in the way it once did.[2]

Why would this be? While correlation does not prove causation, I'm nonetheless struck that this change follows quickly on the heels of the advent of the digital world. I submit that the past few decades have seen a fundamental, age-defining shift in the way humans relate to each other, information, the world around us, and ourselves. The past twenty years have seen the advent of the smartphone, the proliferation of the internet, the democratization of the press, the dawn of social media, the rise of eBay, Amazon, and Google, and the birth of the post-9/11 world order. To be sure, any twenty- or thirty-year period would include many changes. But in the late twentieth and early twenty-first centuries, we've seen not simply another small advance along the arc of history, but the type of epochal, tectonic shift that occurs once every few hundred years.

In many ways, the advent of the digital age has been a boon for society—especially for those who previously felt invisible. On a day-to-day level, one only has to consider the myriad things replaced by a smartphone—seriously, make a list sometime—to recognize how much easier this age has made our lives. And on a societal level, we can look at the scrutiny awoken by the #metoo movement or the magnification of a million marginalized voices through YouTube and TikTok to acknowledge the deep ways this era has made the world a more equitable place.

Even so, we must recognize that the ways in which the digital era shapes us are nuanced, complex, and ever-changing. We cannot easily say that all its effects are "good." If we try to make an inventory of its effects for good and ill, we quickly recognize that the answer is deeply complicated.

Even as someone who is barely old enough to remember a world not ruled by smartphones and the internet, I recognize that true digital natives process the world fundamentally differently than I do. For them, the digital cloud extends the scope of their physiologic brains. Part of the reason separation from their phones is so difficult is because the information they store in their brains and the information they store digitally becomes messy at the borders—no crisp margin divides them.

Futurists have long wondered when humans might become cyborgs, with parts of our native physiology replaced by computers and micromachines. Well, smartphones have at least started the process. Think of how much your phone does for you, how innately you rely on it, and how quickly you grow desperate without it. You may not be physiologically connected to it—you do not share a blood supply or the same oxygen molecules—but many young people may as well be. The smartphone has become an ever-present technological companion and in so doing has become technology's first extension of selfhood.

This invention has fundamentally changed the way we acquire knowledge. Imagine if, in 1980, I had wanted to familiarize myself with the country of Tunisia. I would have started by reading the brief entry in the *Encyclopedia Britannica*. Then, I would have *walked to the library* and used the card catalog to find where the books on Tunisia were shelved, and then checked out the books and carted them home (or briefly perused them there). If I wanted to record specific information from such a book, I would have needed to either transcribe it by hand or make a photocopy. If, after returning the books, I thought, *Oh, I remember this one interesting thing from the book, but I can't remember the details, what was it again?*—I would have needed to actually return to the library and rehash that entire process.

To many young people, the above may seem like a hoax—but that's really how things were.

Now, the price of acquiring knowledge has fallen so far that carrying facts in our brain seems nearly superfluous—but it was not always so. When I was in medical school—just fifteen years ago—I learned facts with the assumption that I would really need to have them memorized. There was a possibility that some patient down the road would present us with a mysterious constellation of symptoms requiring a real Sherlock—with a brain full of facts—to recognize them. Today, in the age of Google and chatGPT, such worries seem downright anachronistic, like pulling out a pocket watch from the vest of a three-piece suit.

That all is not to suggest that doctors don't know things. Most of us still have large catalogs of knowledge at our command. What has changed, instead, is *what it means to know*. Today, "knowing" may as well mean being in command of finding something on the internet as much as having a fact reside in one of your own neurons. The way doctors view ourselves now very much jumps out of *Star Trek*: a large percentage of "my" brain consists of my own neurons, but another portion consists of the neurons provided by UpToDate, Google, and PubMed.

What does all of this have to do with how we understand the gospel?

Everything.

When I was growing up, most Church members were unfamiliar with complex matters of Church history and doctrine. Now, virtually every young person can access such information easily. Not all young people become immersed in challenging questions of Church history and doctrine—some simply have no interest. But those who have even a passing curiosity need nothing more than a smartphone to dive deeply into nearly any question.

None of this is to suggest that the questions people have about the Church are new—in fact, virtually all of them have been around for a long time, and some people have been puzzling over them for decades. But the coming of the internet has put these questions much more front and center—and the "answers" the internet provides are often shorn of context and presented as clear, straightforward, and definitive, when most such conclusions require great nuance and historical rigor to understand appropriately. Moreover, because the internet has changed what it means to know, and because so much of what we do as Church members has to do with trying to know spiritual things, the ascent of the internet has a fundamental effect on the way we understand religion and ourselves. That evolution is important to know as you think about how you ponder spiritual things.

DISTRUSTING AUTHORITY

To begin this section, I'm going to tell you something that may shock you: in the mid-twentieth century, the majority of people in the United States thought the federal government was doing a good job and the prevailing mood in the country was one of trusting authority of all kinds.[3] There was a dominant—though certainly not universal—sentiment that people in authority had good motives and were generally competent and effective.

Well.

If that world sounds as unfamiliar as the one where we used to have to walk to a library to find information, it's because this facet of life, too, has changed significantly over the last half century or so, during which time, almost regardless of the venue of life, our collective, cultural trust in institutions has waned, if not nearly disappeared entirely.

As just one example of this trend, let's look at the way trust in government in the United States has declined over the past sixty years. Starting in 1958, Pew has asked people whether they trust the government to do what's right all or most of the time. In the first year they asked this question, the number responding yes was nearly eighty percent. Eighty percent! Since then, the number has declined almost without exception. Furthermore, while it's true that the numbers vary somewhat between generations, and while there is a bit of an exception between like partisans (e.g., Democrats trust more when a Democratic administration is in power), the trend is strikingly universal in that now even Republicans don't trust a Republican administration and vice versa. Today the percentage is stuck at around twenty.[4]

That drop—from 80 percent in 1958 to 20 percent in 2022— might leave our jaws on the floor.

You might think, *Well, sure the trust in government has dropped*

during that time—look at what the _____ *administration has done"*
(you can fill in the blank according to your partisan leanings). But
that's not anywhere near the whole story. Trust in just about every
institution has dropped. Gallup asks a similar question about the
public's trust in the press as an arbiter of truth. In 1972, the first
year they asked the question, 72 percent of people said they generally trusted the press. More recently, in 2016, that number had
fallen all the way to 32 percent.[5] I could list other examples. The
point is that Americans have generally come to trust institutions
and their leaders much less. The decline of trust in institutions
matters.

The years just after World War II serve as a symbol of the age
when Americans used to trust each other and those who led and informed them. Veterans returning from World War II, for instance,
were almost universally lauded. Belonging to a company for the
entirety of one's working life was not only common, but also seen
as a net good—the evident loyalty was a virtue. Participation in
organized religion was high, as was involvement in civic organizations. Furthermore, there was sense, almost unimaginable today,
that conformity was a pretty good thing.

How we got from there to here is a complicated story, but the
1960s symbolize a large part of the transition. That period seemed
to be the decade when the reigning cultural paradigm went from
celebrating quieter conformists to honoring rabble-rousing radicals.
Virtually everything the 1960s came to celebrate was, in one way
or another, a way of the culture thumbing its nose at the establishment. It wasn't just that we weren't going to trust the establishment
anymore; we were going to overthrow it. The Hippie movement,
the coming of rock and roll, the sexual liberation movement, on
and on—all of these were markers of the waning of the power of
establishments over regular people, and a newfound willingness

of citizens to "speak truth to power."[6] While some version of acceptance of conformity made a comeback in the 1980s with the Reagan Revolution, the 1960s set the tone for the subsequent decades, and our love for individualism and anti-authoritarianism has only been accelerated and facilitated by the digital revolution.

We are still a nation that celebrates independence. Our mantras include sayings like, "Be your own person," "You do you," and "Find your own truth." Obviously, living in a culture where these represent some of the main ways of thinking about the world is going to have profound effects on how we see our relationship to ourselves, God, and the world.

LIVING EACH OTHER'S STORIES

Amid all this discussion of historical context, it is important to note that life inside The Church of Jesus Christ of Latter-day Saints has always been easier for some people than for others. If you are a straight white man with even a slight inclination toward religion, life in the Church can easily be fulfilling, expansive, and intuitive. If, however, you are gay, or Black, or a woman, or single, or an immigrant, or imprisoned, or any of a long list of other identities—then life inside the Church can be much more difficult. I am not suggesting that those who belong to any of those groups cannot find fulfillment within the Church. I *am* saying, however, that fulfillment may not be as straightforward. Further, because our identities and experiences differ so dramatically from each other, and because they so foundationally determine how we experience reality—and the Church—we should take great care in judging anyone, especially when their identities differ markedly from our own.

One benefit to the profound shifts we've experienced in how information is obtained and processed: the world—and the

Church—now show more sensitivity to the struggles of people who have more challenging experiences.

In the 1950s and 1960s, and perhaps even into the 1980s, not only was access to information much more limited than it is now, but the presentation of that information was more tightly controlled. This control was perhaps most apparent in the delivery of "the news." In the 1950s and 1960s, a large percentage of Americans received their news from trusted, seemingly omniscient television network news anchors like Edward R. Murrow and Walter Cronkite. In a way that is difficult for many moderns to imagine, the news as delivered by these men (and they were virtually all men) was accepted not as one perspective among many, but largely as *the ways things were*. That such an overarching narrative dominated the newscape profoundly shaped the way people in the United States understood the flow of current events. And that control was also inherently limiting, as we shall discuss.[7]

These newscasters wielded enormous—if perhaps under-recognized—cultural power. While other voices have always been out there, the newscasters controlled the flow of our national narrative—with all the bias and blind spots such control involved—to a degree we can hardly imagine.

The twenty-first century, on the other hand, has been an entirely different matter. Though the digital revolution has often fallen short in fulfilling its promises and ideals, it has inarguably made the world a more transparent place. Social media empowers people to tell their stories. If much of history has featured tales about old straight white men—and a press whose controls were most often wielded by those same people—the twenty-first century has seen the proliferation of microphones such that now anyone with access to Facebook, Instagram, Twitter/X, or TikTok can insert her or his narrative into our understanding of how the world works. Even so, it's not as if we've welcomed a panacea: the algorithms controlling what we see and hear still often operate with unacknowledged bias that perpetuates prejudice.

This proliferation of counter-narratives has yielded some of the most sweeping and dramatic cultural changes in history. While true causality is difficult to prove, it seems to me intuitive that this is largely responsible for the flourishing of multiple social movements that have ascended over the last fifty years, with the LGBTQ-rights movement as perhaps the most recent and well-known example. Whereas previously those who controlled the national narrative could largely exclude gay voices, today such systematic exclusion would be impossible.

With the proliferation of empowered gay voices came a recognition that gay people do not threaten straight people. The sea of change that has swept the country and many parts of the world on related societal questions—Should a business be able to fire a man because he is gay? Should two gay people be allowed to marry? Should homosexual sex be illegal?—has been stunning and incredibly fast[8]. And I would submit it has come, at least in part, because gay people have finally been able to tell their stories.

Stories move us and lead to sweeping cultural change. And we are seeing similar effects as we share stories more easily—and powerfully—in the Church.

In previous eras, those who did not fit into the Church's more comfortable molds were largely atomized—cut off from each other and without a way to share their stories with the wider Church membership. Long-standing publications, such as *Dialogue* and *Exponent II*, tried to address this atomization (and still exist, making space for and honoring many kinds of voices), but they had limited circulation and less appeal to the sometimes skeptical mainstream members. Now, with the dominance of social media, podcasting, blogging, and all the rest, every person is the president of her or his own publishing company.

In the Church, the accelerated dissemination of information has acted with profound power and to deep and lasting impact. Learning each other's stories—and most especially the stories of the historically marginalized—seems to me to be changing the way we understand ourselves, our country, our world, and our religion.

LIFE IN A ROOM WITH A THOUSAND FRACTURED MIRRORS

All of us largely understand ourselves through the reflections we see in mirrors held up to us by our family, our friends, and society. We largely come to a sense of our own identity by learning from how others talk about, understand, and portray us. We are especially susceptible to this type of suggestion when we are young—but most of us never really grow out of it. It's just wired into our psychology.

But here's the thing: the digital age has shattered all the mirrors.

In 2022, psychology professor Jonathan Haidt wrote an insightful article provocatively titled, "Why the Past 10 Years of American Life Have Been Uniquely Stupid."[9] In it, he argues that the ubiquitous rise of social media has entirely transformed the way we look at each other and ourselves, and, in particular, the way we communicate with others.

One of his key insights is that social media has armed every person with a "digital BB gun." The gun is usually not powerful enough to kill someone, but it can absolutely harm others, and it is really, really good at breaking things down. That explanation makes sense if you think about Twitter/X. By definition, posts can contain only 280 characters. Yes, you can write a thread, but that's not really what Twitter was built for. It specializes in bites of information, not in articulation, explanation, or argument.

This all came home to me vividly in mid-2022 when I was attending a medical conference. I had made a conscious decision just before going that I was going to be more active on Twitter during the conference. The most important part of these conferences for me, as a cancer doctor, is the presentation of new data. Because I have expertise in GI cancers, I decided before going that I would tweet concise summaries and analyses of each new data set that was presented within my specialty. I figured doing so was a meaningful way to disseminate helpful, contextualized information to those who either couldn't come at all or who didn't have the expertise to place this new data in context.

I tagged each of my posts appropriately and labeled them in real time. But what caught my attention was that almost none of them got any kind of meaningful response or engagement. At the same time, however, I noted that during one of the sessions, the panel invited to discuss the data was composed of all men. I snapped a photo and wrote, "Hey [conference organizers], I can't help but notice that something is missing from this panel, can't quite put my finger on it, but . . ."[10]

And *that* tweet was the viral one, racking up over four hundred likes, extensive comments, and many retweets.

Let me be clear: I thought that tweet was valuable. I tweeted it with the hashtag "#heforshe" for a reason. But at the same time, the other Twitter threads I posted, some of which contained life-saving information, got no attention. My point here is that Twitter is made for things like that tweet: teeny bites of provocative information. The ideas that gain the most traction on Twitter almost always pack an emotional punch—the medium favors quick, visceral statements and often largely ignores reasoned, careful discourse.

Similarly, it is better at tearing things down than at building them up. Indeed, in that sense we might say that Twitter/X is a technology entirely apropos to its time: it reflects the people who use it in that we are *all* much better at tearing down than we are at building up.

We live in an era of deconstruction.

Furthermore, many of us have become *obsessed* with using our Facebook/Twitter/etc. as BB guns. Even those who don't use them at all still *live in the world that is created when they are used all the time*. Modern technologies have so thoroughly deconstructed so much of the world—it's as though forty years ago we lived in a hall of mirrors where we would look around to see our own reflections and learn who we were, but now the mirrors have all been shattered, and it is hard to see much of anything.

This all matters profoundly because the Church gives us meaning, in part, by providing substantive narratives to help us understand who we are and what we mean and by helping us build community—but those two forces, narrative and community, are deeply wounded in the world of social media. Many young people who go to college come to question the Church precisely because, often for the first time, they face in all its relentless fury the onslaught of those deconstructing BBs. It can be profoundly disorienting when all the mirrors shatter—it may seem that our sense of self, community, and the world has been shattered, too.

While the world created by Twitter is profoundly good at breaking things down, it is not nearly as good at—and sometimes is entirely incapable of—building anything up to fill the resulting void.

The last couple of decades, then, have seen the world transformed. While it's easy enough to see how that transformation has come via multiple technologies, it is even more important to recognize that those same changes have also transformed the way we understand ourselves and the ways in which we relate to others. Because the digital revolution has so dramatically shifted such basic concepts as what it means to know, it should hardly surprise us that it has changed both what we think about religion and how we develop our religious sense. When we couple these technological shifts with the rising tide of anti-authoritarianism, we should hardly be surprised that the first few decades of our new century have made it significantly harder to believe in any organized religion. Indeed, a yawning divide has opened up regarding how religion is understood by previous generations and how it is understood by millennials and Gen Z.

2

WHO NEEDS CHURCH, ANYWAY?

Questions

- What good is organized religion? Can't I just be spiritual on my own?
- Who needs scriptures?
- Does belonging to the Church narrow or expand my ability to love?
- How can attending church add nuance and depth to my personal ethics?

The first time I really went car shopping was when I was thirty-six (before that I had purchased only used cars from family members on the cheap).

Our family was growing, and so we needed a bigger car. I drove to most car dealerships within thirty miles of our house and listened to pitch after pitch about speed and special features, ratings, and resale value. It was all fine, but after a while I realized something important: *I just didn't care.* We were lucky to live in northern California, and on most days I rode my bike to work, and still do. I loved bike riding because it was quiet and smooth and gave me time to think. So, for all the convincing pitches of those many salespeople, a car just seemed unnecessary and I really wasn't interested.

I think that for some young people, church is kind of like that.

These people may have lots of reasons for feeling this way. They may not like the politics they associate with church. They may not feel they fit in at church. They may feel church excludes them or those they love. They may question whether churches prioritize the things that are most important. Or, like I did while shopping for a car, they may simply not feel drawn or compelled toward the necessity of the thing in the first place. For these latter people, the problem is not finding the *right* church, but rather understanding why a church matters at all. So, before we address anything about the journey of faith, the beauty of the restored Church, or any of the rest of it, it seems like we should probably start by exploring why church might be worth valuing at all.

THE PROBLEM WITH CHURCH

In many important ways, church increasingly seems like an outdated concept. It's just kind of, well, a twentieth-century thing, like radio, mixtapes, dial-up modems, and Walkman cassette players. This sense holds sway among the young and can create deep rifts within families because, while older Americans tend to be overtly religious, the young overall are much less so. It is possible that this phenomenon is purely a function of age—perhaps the young will ripen into more religious people as they age—yet based on research from both Pew and the *Next Mormons Survey* by Jana Riess, such does not seem to be the case.

The question, though, is why?

Part of the answer has to do with the way our culture is shifting over time, as discussed in Chapter 1. There is significant research to indicate that we in the United States are simply a less communitarian people than we used to be. Robert Putnam's *Bowling Alone* famously described this shift and attributed the drift to cultural changes like the rise of television and other individualistic media. These tendencies have only intensified over recent decades, as research from Jean Twenge and Sherry Turkle on the social effects of the internet attests. Thus part of the reason church seems anachronistic is because the idea of going to the same place every week to meet with the same group of people over and over may just seem a little outdated.

But the discomfort goes far beyond this.

Another factor that plays an important role is the often-uncomfortable marriage of religion and American politics. It may surprise some young readers to know that in many prior eras there was little formal—or even informal—connection between political parties and religion, or between religion and politics in general. Around the time of the election of Ronald Reagan, however, a group of influential evangelical leaders formed coalitions like *Focus on the Family,* whose explicit purpose was to gather and wield political influence. Whereas previously the strong thought among the religious had been to render to Caesar what was Caesar's and to God what was God's,[1] now the idea was instead to use Caesar's influence to try to advance God's objectives (as that group of religious leaders understood those objectives). This is a simplification of complex history, but there is truth to the idea that secular/political marriage is relatively new.

It was one thing when these political-religious alliances came to fruition during the presidencies of George W. Bush and Ronald Reagan, who, whatever else we might say about them, both seemed to have genuine and long-held spiritual beliefs. This trend has reached a startling and strange peak, however, with the alliance between Donald Trump and the religious right. Few would dispute that Donald Trump is the least personally religious president in recent memory. Even so, evangelical Christians are likely his single most unwaveringly supportive constituency.

The union between the political right and evangelical Christianity has driven young people away from church in at least two fashions. First, because of the strength and prominence of the union, many churches in the U.S. have come to be associated with anything that comes out of the right wing of U.S. politics. The relationship has become so close that, fairly or not, many young people may look at the right-wing pundits of the world and say to themselves, "If that's what church means, I'm not interested." Secondly, many young members of various Christian churches may look at the conduct of political leaders in general—and at their treatment of the vulnerable in particular—and say, "If my religion supports those politicians, then I can't comfortably stay any longer."

My point here is very close to the one the Church, at least implicitly, makes every four years—or even more often. The Church teaches consistently, even insistently, that there are positive gospels ideals to be found in all major political parties. But when a church—or the very idea of church—becomes so closely associated with a particular political movement that they are seen as virtually the same, modern culture can then nail the failings of the political party onto the church as well.

This tarnishing, fair or not, drives away young people who do not want to belong to the associated political parties.

Even beyond that tarnishing, however, is this quandary: I believe many young people don't understand the purpose of church in a large, existential sense. Many young people consider themselves "spiritual" but not "religious." And it's worth considering what this distinction might entail. The differences between living a spiritual and a religious life seem to amount to the following: a religious person adheres to a particular code of conduct prescribed by a church, while a spiritual person defines her own moral code. A religious person belongs to a consistent community, while a spiritual person is free to move about any, or none. Finally, a religious person stakes a claim on a specific set of spiritual beliefs, often articulated in sacred texts, while a spiritual person claims no such specific allegiance.

In short, on the surface, the question of being religious is one of commitment—to people, to standards, to words, and to a religious way of being.

And yet, this all brings us to a final way in which church ill suits many young people. It's not just that they believe institutional religion is wedded to a specific political party in which they cannot find comfort. No, in an ironic twist, what most worries many young people I know is that they fear institutional religion has lost its moral compass and, in so doing, not only no longer merits their fidelity but makes actively supporting the Church an immoral act. In other words, a young person looks at our Church (or any of many other churches, for that matter) and says, "The movement for LGBTQ rights is the Civil Rights movement of our time, and I feel *deeply* that securing equal rights for my LGBTQ friends is a fundamental moral cause—so if the Church can't support that, then I can't support the Church." I believe this personal moral fervor likely underlies another basic cultural challenge in terms of millennial and Gen-Z Church participation: they have become so accustomed to frustration with this or that moral stance from their leaders that they now bristle against the very idea of spiritual authority.

This vital point thus follows. The strawman suggesting that people leave the Church because of moral laxity often gets it exactly backward: many people don't leave because they want license to do wrong—they leave because they need the Church to speak up more forcefully in support of the very moral causes that matter most deeply to them. Now, to be clear, I am writing this book in part because I believe there are other angles to be considered on all of these questions—and that we can seek to offer Church leaders and even the Church itself a measure of grace, as well—but I have spoken to enough young people about these matters to understand how deeply these concerns speak to their souls.

In light of that all: why would a modern twenty-something want to belong to—let alone really try to participate meaningfully in—a church like ours, or any church for that matter? It is to these questions we will now turn.

WORDS TO LIVE BY

One of the most definitive aspects of most world religions is that they have a set of sacred texts. This tendency is so pronounced that even George Lucas's Jedi Knights have them. Such sacred texts, as the designation implies, function on a higher plane than normal literature. We may derive great benefit from—and might even become better people because of—a novel by F. Scott Fitzgerald or a poem by Mary Oliver, but many of us sense intuitively that even these great works fundamentally differ from scripture. So why should scripture comprise a meaningful part of our spiritual lives?

I ask this question in part because our modern era (or perhaps every era) does few things so well as it demonstrates the truth of

Shylock's maxim: "The devil can cite scripture for his purpose."[2] The Bible, perhaps the most revered book in the history of literature and scripture, has nonetheless been wielded to justify actions such as slavery and stoning. Beyond even those dramatic and extreme examples, we've all seen modern demonstrations of what Joseph Smith described during the Second Great Awakening as a "war of words and tumult of opinions" (Joseph Smith—History 1:10). Scripture can be wielded as a weapon every bit as fierce as a sword.

Furthermore, scriptures have come to seem anachronistic. In at least one sense this characteristic is literally and inescapably true—depending on what one accepts as scripture, even our relatively young canon deals mostly with events from around 200 years ago; in most religions, the events depicted occurred millennia ago. But more recently, with our modern exposure to science and our post-modern suspicion of meta-narratives in general, the scriptures have come to seem like relics from a prior era.

So, if we accept all of this as true, then why resort to scripture at all?

The answer, I think, is that God's word gives ballast to our spiritual ship as we sail the seas of life. In ancient sailing, ballast consisted of heavy material—such as rocks—placed in the bottom of a boat to stabilize the ship amid roiling seas. Such a stabilizing weight is initially counterintuitive—what could be less helpful to a ship trying to stay afloat than something literally weighing it down? But it turns out that without such weighty cargo, a ship becomes unstable and unmoored, liable to float to and fro with every wind or current that arises.

Even considering the vagaries of how limited our understanding of scripture is, I would argue that scripture takes on the same function for us in life. Our best intentions notwithstanding, without scripture we are subject to rise and fall with every ebb and swell, inevitably tossed about on a sea of opinions and cultural currents that make it hard to chart a course safely home. I am not saying that we subscribe to scriptural inerrancy—we explicitly do not. I am instead suggesting that it blesses our spiritual lives to take scripture *seriously*. Consider Fatimah Salleh and Margaret Hemming Olsen's multivolume *The Book of Mormon for the Least of These*. These books do not simply recite scripture and take it to mean what its most superficial interpretation suggests—they instead wrestle scripture, including the most difficult parts, to pry from it substance and succor that would not otherwise appear on a superficial reading. These authors—and others like them—teach us something important about a way in which we too often misunderstand the very purpose and design of scripture. Too often, I fear, we come to think of scripture like a divine instruction manual, as if we could open the pages and read off a list of "11 easy steps you can take to be really happy."

But scripture just isn't like that.

Choose your canonical volume and what you will *not* find is a story of people leading nearly perfect lives and receiving in exchange bliss and never-ending happiness. Instead, you find pages populated by complex, multifaceted characters who very much want and try to do what's right, but who often find that life is filled with choices between what is good and what is ever better, or between what is bad and what is ever worse. What's more, we find scriptural protagonists who are acutely aware of both their own shortcomings and the full weight and splendor of God's glory and who, therefore, tremble at the task set before them: to try to capture in words the meaning and full beauty of the divine. These are people who want desperately to deliver the message they feel charged by history and providence to share but who worry constantly that they will be unable to fully capture or convey. They seem always to be aware of the gap that stretches between the ideal of what they proclaim and the reality of their lives and the world around them.

To give a bit of weight to my own thoughts here, let's consider the U.S. Declaration of Independence. In recent years, this document has come to be seen with suspicion because Thomas Jefferson—the declaration's chief author—was unquestionably hypocritical in that he enslaved people and held many harmful notions regarding racial superiority. Thus, a modern student can fairly ask, *What good is a document boldly declaring the importance of inalienable rights and universal equality if it was written by an enslaver?*

But that's just it. The answer—unquestionably a paradox—underlines the very importance of the document and the inevitable spiritual power of its words. If you look at the moments of greatest rhetorical weight in our nation's history, virtually all of them reference the Declaration implicitly, and a good majority of them quote it explicitly. When Abraham Lincoln spoke at Gettysburg, he spoke of a "new nation, conceived in Liberty, and dedicated to the proposition that all men are created equal." He then went on to frame the Civil War and the fight against slavery as the battle for the preservation of the very unmet ideals that the Declaration enshrines, and committed "that from these honored dead we take increased devotion to that cause for which they gave the last full measure of devotion."[3] Likewise, when Martin Luther King Jr. spoke from the steps of the Lincoln Memorial, he spoke of "the magnificent words" of the Declaration and the Constitution, and then referenced them as a promissory note that subsequent generations had left unfulfilled and that he and his compatriots had gone to the National Mall to claim—that they together wanted to "make real the promises of democracy."[4] And when Barack Obama spoke at the Philadelphia Constitution Center on race in America, he again turned to America's founding. He described "a Constitution that had at its very core the ideal of equal citizenship under the law; a Constitution that promised its people liberty, and justice, and a union that could be and should be perfected over time"—but then went on to recognize that the words alone were not enough: "What would be needed were Americans in successive generations who were willing to do their part—through protests and struggle, on the streets and in the courts, through a civil war and civil disobedience and always at great risk—to narrow that gap between the promise of our ideals and the reality of their time."[5]

With that line, then-candidate Obama struck perhaps the most important function that the country's founding texts play in our civil lives—and that scriptures play in our spiritual ones. The point of the Declaration is not that there was no gap between the ideals it enshrines and the reality of the lives of the men who wrote it. No, the point is that there *was*—and still is—a gap.

But the words beckon us to shrink it.

That's just it—not in spite of but because of the gap, the words really, really matter.

When we look at our own scripture, the gap presses on us so firmly that it may make us uncomfortable. What about the gap between 2 Nephi 26:33 and the reality of our church's history with respect to race? What about our insistence in general conference that women are equal when we hear fewer women's voices in those same conferences? Add the large space between what I am and what scripture tells me I should be, and it is suddenly easy, amid these gaping spaces, to feel as though we should give up the entire enterprise.

But my feeling is that that very moment—when faced with the great distance between where we are and where we want to be—is when scripture matters the most. That very moment is when we can allow scripture to give voice to the angels of our better natures, beckoning us to a higher plane.

GETTING PAST "US" VS. "THEM"

Because I teach at a medical school, I spend a lot of time counseling with those who are getting ready to enter medicine. I recently spent time talking with one such young man who was as extraordinary a medical school applicant as I've ever met. Coming from a disadvantaged background and having grown up in something of a fractured family, he pressed through college with a perfect GPA and scored perfectly—yes, perfectly—on the MCAT. In addition, he had participated in multiple meaningful community-service initiatives and had set himself up in just about every way to impress the socks off an admissions committee. Not surprisingly, after applications were submitted and interviews finished, he received offers of admission from just about every place he applied and full-ride scholarships to some of the country's best-known medical colleges.

We had become friends by the time these offers came in, and so the first thing I did when he informed me of each invitation from a new school was to celebrate and congratulate. Once all the admissions were counted, however, we went to lunch one day, and I looked him in the eyes and said, "It's so wonderful that you will get this opportunity that is so vanishingly rare. I really couldn't be happier for you. Now, however, we need to have a talk about *how to not become a jerk*—and one of your best guards against that is to make sure you consistently attend church."

Now, you need to understand that this is a young man—let's call him Andrew—who is anything but a jerk. Indeed, in all my interactions with him, I've never found him to be anything but bright, engaging, deferential, and kind. Why, then, would I give him this advice? Because medical school, especially at a place many view as "elite," has a way of making you see the world as being composed of "our kind of people" and "that kind of people." Having spent many years in various universities over the last decades, I've seen the insidious ways this mentality can rust a person's soul. From the very first day of orientation, it begins: "We are proud," a dean of the school will say, "to have gathered here the most impressive and diverse group of first-year medical students ever to grace this campus . . ." And so it goes.

None of that is unique to medical school. Similar things could be said at any college, law school, or business school throughout the country. What's more, this mentality isn't even distinct to school. Humans love to divvy ourselves up into various "us"es and "them"s. We do it in politics. We do it based on economics. We do it based on where we live. The point is that we seem almost hardwired to search for reasons to think we are better than—though we often call it being "different from"—the people we call "other." (And, of course, we Church members tell on ourselves when we fall into the tired habit of divvying the world into "members" and "nonmembers," as if everyone in the world but us should be defined by what they are not.)

And this brings us to what *can* be one of the most important functions of church communities—they can repudiate any sense of superiority or otherness. Unfortunately, we are not perfect at embracing that repudiation. Members of many different minority groups can recount deeply saddening stories of having been "othered" by local congregations or by the institutional Church. If we are not careful, we can even fall into the sorry state of the Zoramites, who chiefly saw Church membership itself as a badge of honor meant to distinguish them from their inferior (because they did not belong to the same church) brethren. But the thing about our weekly worship is that we are down in the trenches with those we might otherwise see as others—and experience shows that it is much more difficult to dislike someone you are baking with, nursery-ing with, laughing with, crying with, teaching, loving, and being taught by. Whatever walls we construct between ourselves tend to come tumbling down when we work together.

In this vein, our congregations have a leg up on even many of our supposedly more broad-minded cultural institutions. In 2016, Peggy Noonan, a weekly columnist at *The Wall Street Journal* and former presidential speechwriter, wrote an article in which she said that modern politics are increasingly being defined by the difference not between races or socioeconomic classes but instead between the "protected" and the "unprotected": "The protected make public policy. The unprotected live in it. The unprotected are starting to push back, powerfully. The protected are the accomplished, the secure, the successful—those who have power or access to it. They are protected from much of the roughness of the world. More to the point, *they are protected from the world they have created.*"[6] What Ms. Noonan was getting at here, I think, was a fundamental disconnect in our culture and thereby in our politics between the rhetoric of those making policy and the fact that they do not actually have to live with the consequences of that policy because they are insulated from real life.

If our wards work the way they should (and we always have work to do better), the protected and the unprotected will be living, worshiping, and serving together—indeed, in a ward, neither such distinction should define anybody. I recognize that here, too, a gap often yawns widely. Wards, sadly, can be places for cliques and social strife, but in their best iteration—the ideal toward which we strive, even recognizing the gap that remains—wards can deeply bless us and provide a refuge, a haven for all types of believers.

LEARNING COMPLEX MORALITY

One final—and perhaps counterintuitive—benefit of organized religion deserves mention here. Jonathan Haidt is a prominent social psychologist who has done as much as any other modern scientist to help answer the question, "Why do people do what they do?" He has determined that the most important answer is that we make decisions at the most basic level by relying on what he calls humanity's moral "foundations." Through conducting hundreds of online and in-person interviews, Haidt and his colleagues have demonstrated that when our subconscious minds react toward or against something, they do so largely based on one or more of six moral axes: care/harm, liberty/oppression, fairness/cheating, loyalty/betrayal, authority/subversion, and sanctity/degradation.[7]

It is probably helpful to unpack a bit of what Haidt is getting at. When he refers to "moral axes," he is not talking just about something we hold up as valuable; he is talking about the measuring stick we use to determine whether an action is moral. For instance, if I tell you that a twelfth-grade teacher chooses 10 percent of her class at random and that those students will be able to use books and notes on an exam while the others will not, you will probably bristle. If I then point out that the other students really shouldn't mind—nothing is being taken from them, and (assuming the class is not graded on a curve) the chosen students doing well does no direct disservice to those who can't have notes—you are likely to conclude, regardless, "Yes, but it's just not fair."

You would be resorting here to the "fairness/cheating" axis. The point is not just that you don't like cheating, but rather that fairness is a standard against which we judge an action's morality.

Similarly, if you were visiting France and saw a man urinating on the side of Chartres Cathedral, you would likely be disturbed. If I asked you why, you might initially try to concoct something about damaging the property and how it's not his to damage. Even if I could assure you, however, that the property would not be durably damaged, you would likely still be troubled and, eventually, would have to admit that the standard against which you are holding the person's behavior is that sacred things should be treated with deference.

Modern life increasingly operates on a limited moral spectrum: especially in "WEIRD" societies (Western, educated, industrialized, rich, and democratic), we are increasingly focusing on the liberty/oppression and care/harm axes to the exclusion of all others. For example, doctor colleagues of mine are likely to nod approvingly if I appeal to "rights" or to "care" as rationale for a decision, but they will just as likely look askance if I base an argument on "sanctity."

In the Church, however, we are more comfortable invoking reasoning from all Haidt's moral axes. In a Church discussion, we could say that we should or should not do something because of a sense of the sacred, or from a commitment to loyalty, or submission to authority—and all of these would at least make sense. The latter axes don't necessarily always win out, but at least they have a chance at the table. Our morality is a complex and nuanced one, and I suspect that much of the ethical friction we feel within ourselves as Church members stems from exactly that: moral axis A rubbing up against moral axis B in a way that occasionally makes us uncomfortable. We are forced, in church, to weigh axis A against axis B and to discern what should win out when B grates against C in a way that skews against D. These are thorny problems—and that's the point.

Please do not misunderstand: I am *not* arguing against the importance of the liberty/oppression and care/harm axes—far from it. What I am saying, however, is that a life constructed by paying attention to virtually only one moral axis runs the risk of becoming unidimensional and ethically untethered. There is something centering and healthy about feeling pulled between this and that ethical impulse. I believe such multidimensional pulling centers us and increases the likelihood we will live ethically substantive lives, working to improve our behavior on multiple moral axes, not just one or two. If we are serious about walking the pathway of restored Christian discipleship, that journey will require us to make difficult decisions that cause us to measure the relative weights of an action's effects along competing moral axes simultaneously. This is a feature, not a bug.

This wrestle matters because it forces us to move outside of ourselves—it forces us to question our own moral intuition. And that questioning matters. Belonging to a church with specific doctrines and commandments is difficult precisely because it will sometimes ask us to consider that we might be wrong. While most religious people belong to their chosen church because its moral compass largely aligns with their own, there will still be times when the compasses don't quite align. This nonalignment can be uncomfortable but also productive.

Those moments of disagreement suggest an important and underlying truth: maybe we don't know everything. In today's world, "to thine own self be true"[8] has become such a truism that it hardly bears articulating. To recommend that a person follow his conscience is about as novel as observing that the sky looks *particularly blue* this morning. But amid a world where individual morality reigns supreme as our culture's lodestar, church reminds us that leaving ourselves to our own moral devices does not constitute a panacea. We are meant to grapple with placing our own moral inclinations up against those articulated by ancient and modern prophets. Doing so forces us to reckon with difficult, sometimes existential, questions that may not confront us if we surrender to accepting our own moral compasses as infallible.

3

WHAT DOES IT MEAN TO BELIEVE?

Questions

- What is the difference between "I believe" and "I know"?
- I feel as though my testimony used to burn more brightly—why would it waver over time?
- What does "doubt" mean?
- What role does doubt play in the journey of belief?

What do we mean when we use words like *believe, faith,* and *doubt?*

It turns out those words are harder to define than you might think. Go ahead, try it. Write down your own definitions. My guess is you'll find it a little tricky. Even if you succeed, try writing the definitions down and then comparing them with those of ten friends of our faith—let alone friends from other faiths.

I teach institute in northern California, and a few years ago I was struck by this same question: What does it mean to know? I threw it out to the class. "Please define it for me," I said. "What does a Church member mean when she says, 'I know'?"

No one had any idea. Or, rather, people assumed they had clear ideas until they really started trying to articulate them. Then they found it much more difficult than they'd expected.

I had a flexible course schedule that semester, so we spent a great deal of time working together as a class to answer the query. What hit me then, however, was that not only were my students (and I) initially unable to readily come up with a definition, but once we began working toward one, we disagreed and our understanding evolved, even over the course of two class periods. This exercise taught me that while the process of knowing is central to the way we understand and experience our religion, there is a great deal about it we don't understand as well as we think.

THE JOURNEY TOWARD
SPIRITUAL KNOWLEDGE

Let's imagine a young college student who was raised in a loving, stable, and mostly nonreligious home. Let's call our young woman Esperanza. One night, in the summer after her sophomore year of college, Esperanza goes camping by herself. After the sun sets, and without a tent, she lies down in her sleeping bag and finds the stars showering her with light. Astonished by their beauty and immediacy, she becomes contemplative, and soon, a *thing* happens. She can't articulate the experience precisely, but she suddenly feels simultaneously swallowed up by the grandeur of the universe and also infinitely important in a way she never had before.

When she gets in her car the next morning, she has become

convinced that what she encountered was God—but she has almost no idea what that means.

Alive with newfound enthusiasm and famished to define divinity, Esperanza rushes the next morning to find a fellow student she vaguely recognizes as religious. She hurries up to the student, explains her experience, and then says, "Look, I hardly know what happened last night, but I need to figure it out. I suddenly believe God exists, but I don't know anything about who God is or what God wants of me—can you help me? I suddenly have so many questions; how do I find the answers?"

And, wouldn't you know it, it turns out Esperanza's friend is a member of our church. Let's say that in the process of their discussion that day, the friend mentions the Book of Mormon to Esperanza and—again, wouldn't you know it?—even happens to have a copy. The friend sends Esperanza home with a copy of the book and an invitation to read it and come to know for herself that it's true.

Esperanza, filled with earnest enthusiasm, sets about trying to do just that.

What does that experience—trying to come to know—look like?

When we consider a person weighing a truth-claim, it's helpful to visualize the process as just that: weighing something in the balance. We can imagine a set of scales: on one side we place anything that supports a claim, and on the other scale we place anything that would refute it.

We can imagine Esperanza, as she makes her way through the book, doing just that. She encounters a strange-seeming historical aspect of the book and places that on the "false" side of the scale, but then she recognizes that the book is important to her friend and places that on the "true" side. When she later prays and feels

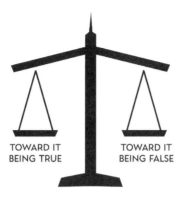

spiritual stirrings around the book, she counts that on the "true" side as well. And so on.

Let's pause for a moment here and talk about those "spiritual stirrings."

Many moderns would object to even including them on the scale. This objection comes for many reasons, including because such stirrings cannot be easily replicated and are not externally verifiable. As Church members, we may feel slightly embarrassed about discussing such feelings, believing they aren't "real" or shouldn't "count." But while this idea seems rigorous or scientific at the outset, its allure fades quickly upon examination.

Now, look. I love science, and I am a big advocate of rigorous evidence. In fact, much of what I do with my patients as a cancer doctor is explaining to them what the best evidence says about what their treatment should be. Still, while the kind of evidence we glean from the scientific method matters enormously and has become one of the unassailable foundations of modern society, we cannot fully benefit from the blessings brought about by utilizing the scientific method unless we also recognize that method's limitations and acknowledge that it is not the mother of everything worth knowing.

The feature that distinguishes knowledge gained through the scientific method is that it must be reproducible and verifiable. That the scientific method demands knowledge with these features is a good thing—we do not want to rely on Dr. So-and-So's "good feelings" to determine the best cancer treatment. Nonetheless, not all important knowledge hews to these requirements.

Many of our decisions—including some of the most important ones—either cannot or should not be made based on externally verifiable (that is, scientific) evidence alone. This principle is true whether we discuss choosing what to have for breakfast, where to attend college, or whom we should marry. Likewise, in establishing the truth or falsity of a spiritual claim, I can certainly seek evidence in archaeological or literary proofs, but I must also pay serious attention to the ineffable.[1]

The next point we need to consider here stands out to me as one of the most important ones we'll discuss precisely because it's one that we so often get wrong: we should not artificially limit the ways in which God speaks to us.

Many of us Church members have a surprisingly simplistic understanding of what "revelation" is supposed to look like. For instance, if I am teaching an institute class and ask, "How can a person come to know the Book of Mormon is true?" I will get bowled over with a chorus of people offering Moroni 10:3–5. I love these verses and have found great meaning in them, but I also believe they can be easily misinterpreted; indeed, many of us use them to demand spiritual ransom from God.

The most common problem in approaching these verses is that they can be interpreted as offering a gumball-machine theology. Children love gumball machines because they are simple, reliable, quick, and offer a treat. If you put in your quarter and turn the crank, a gumball drops out. We often speak of Moroni 10:3–5 in the same way: reading, pondering, and praying are the quarter and the crank-turn, and an emotional experience with the divine is the gumball. Simple as that.

But, of course, discerning spiritual truth seldom occurs so simply, and, even if it did, such experiences rarely constitute the last word on the subject. The gumball-machine formulation is problematic in at least two respects. The first is that it sets an expectation of an immediate answer. This expectation is troublesome because when a sincere seeker of truth encounters these verses, expects an immediate answer, and then doesn't find one forthcoming, she can easily assume that either the whole thing is a sham or that she is spiritually broken and should stop trying—even though neither is the case. The problem in that scenario is the misinterpretation of the verse, not the sincerity or spirituality of the seeker.

The other problem is that we tend to read into this verse an idea that isn't there, or at least that isn't *all* that's there. When speaking of *how* we will discern an answer to a spiritual question, the verse says only that we will know "by the power of the Holy Ghost." My experience indicates most members of the Church are conditioned to add, "by experiencing a certain emotional sensation that we often refer to as a 'burning of the bosom.'" I don't wish to question the validity of such experiences, and indeed, a few of my most-prized encounters with the divine have come in similar ways—but our implicit understanding that we can *assume* the answer will come in that way has left many a seeker of truth frustrated or heartbroken.

I'm reminded of a story a friend told me a few years ago of a college student who came to him in great distress because the student had been searching earnestly but apparently fruitlessly for a confirmation of some spiritual truth. As they discussed his concerns, the young man said, "Everyone keeps telling me that if I read, ponder, and pray, I will get a burning of the bosom—but I'm a scientist, and *my bosom just doesn't burn.*" During the discussion that followed, the young man came to recognize that "so great a cloud of witnesses" surrounded him (Hebrews 12:1), albeit witnesses that didn't happen to be the specific emotional kind he had been expecting. An experience with the "power of the Holy Ghost" can come as an emotional encounter, but it may just as easily be a sudden flash of insight, a deepening of personal empathy, or a greater desire to be like Jesus. The Spirit can spark creative energy, illuminate a thorny intellectual problem, or bridge a connection that had hitherto remained obscure.

We should not artificially limit the ways in which God speaks to us.

Okay, now back to the scales.

The balance between the scale favoring truth and the scale favoring falsity will likely shift again and again. We expect them to vary over time as experiences grow or shrink in importance, as new evidence comes to light, and as the interpretation of past knowledge and experiences takes on additional nuance. That is to say: knowledge is not (or at least is not always) a yes/no proposition. I may be relatively more certain of a claim today than I was yesterday, but my relative certainty about that claim may wane again tomorrow.

With that idea in mind, I'd like to introduce what may seem like a strange idea: charting the rise and fall of spiritual certainty on a graph. As the balance between the positive and negative scales varies over time, we can graph their movement, with time on the x-axis and the person's assessment of how likely the claim is to be true on the y-axis. If the "true" scale weighs more heavily than the "false" scale, the line moves up; if the negative scale weighs more heavily, the line moves down.

Now, a couple of points about these graphs. First, the graphs are not complex—they're just an attempt to illustrate something that can be hard to visualize. Second, these graphs are good only so far as they help. If they don't work for you, that's fine. And even if they do, in a later chapter I'm going to return to their fundamental limitation and point out why they are quite problematic. But I hope they'll be useful for now.

Let's return to Esperanza. Imagine that after her conversation with her friend, she begins to read the Book of Mormon earnestly. What might happen next? How might we imagine and graph the experience she will have?

We'll look at three examples—just a few culled from an infinite array of possibilities (which I will talk about and deconstruct later). Here is the first:

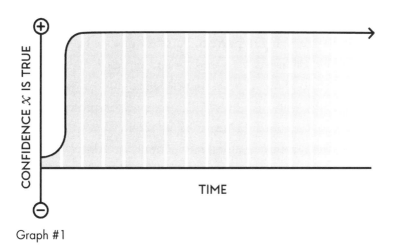

Graph #1

In this example, Esperanza spends relatively little time at the get-go with her faith increasing minimally and incrementally. Soon thereafter, however—perhaps as she finishes the book and has a remarkable spiritual outpouring while praying to know it is true—there is a sudden jump in the graph: her personal evaluation of the evidence makes a quantum leap. What's more, after that initial quantum leap, her evaluation of the evidence remains essentially constant perpetually.

We will discuss this graph as compared to the others below further along, but for now I wish only to point out that many of us expect the development of a testimony to look like this and only this—and that expectation is a problem. For example, I fear that a misunderstanding of our missionaries' invitations can lead to precisely this wrong expectation. Not to harp on Moroni 10:3–5, but misunderstanding those verses can get us into real trouble. If we believe those verses mean that every truth-seeker can expect something like Graph #1, we set ourselves up for the possibility of self-manipulation, false expectation, and frustration. Because cultural expectations for gaining a testimony are so strong, we may try to wrestle mild spiritual feelings into an overwhelming witness because we are trying to prove to ourselves that we have received just the kind of answer we hoped for and expected. We might do well to instead allow spiritual knowledge to come as we've been told it usually will: "line upon line, precept upon precept, here a little, and there a little" (2 Nephi 28:30; see also Isaiah 28:10), or, to cite scripture's most beautiful metaphor on the subject, as subtly, silently, and slowly "as the dews from heaven" (D&C 121:45). The point of quoting these verses is to highlight the way in which they complicate and expand what we learn in Moroni 10:3–5—while those Moroni verses matter, they are nowhere near the scriptures' last word on the subject.

A second alternative might look like Graph #2.

If Esperanza had this graph as her own, her process of knowing would be much less dramatic than in Graph #1. Indeed, if her graph looked like this one and we asked her somewhere far down the road, "So, when did you develop your testimony?" she might

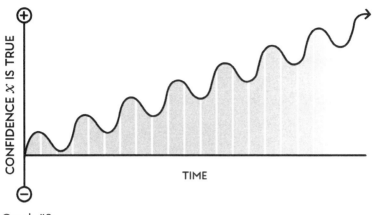

Graph #2

pause, think about it for a few minutes, and respond honestly, "I don't really know." Further, unlike Graph #1, this one features ebbs and swells as part and parcel of the knowing process. One day she may feel surer, the next day less so. And never does she experience anything like a quantum leap. With my hat tipped to Elder David A. Bednar, this graph looks more like the light that comes slowly at dawn, and nothing like lightning or even the turning on of a bulb.[2]

If Esperanza's path to knowing looks like Graph #3 on the following page, she's in for something of a bumpy ride. Here, she might experience something like a quantum leap not just once, but two or three times—and in this case, quantum descents accompany the leaps and are every bit as real and visceral. Perhaps she has a few of those lightning-like experiences where her spiritual knowledge rockets upward, but just as surely knows the dizzying sensation of watching her confidence plummet, with all the fear and nausea that dip entails.

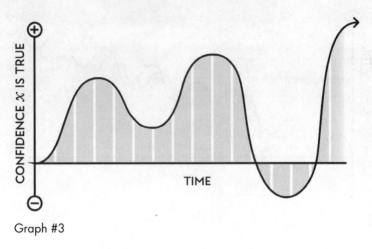

Graph #3

FAITH AND KNOWLEDGE

With these simplified graphs in mind, we can proceed to defining two of the most important words relating to gaining spiritual knowledge. I would suggest that:

1) To *know* is to accept a truth-claim when compelled to do so by overwhelming evidence in favor of the claim.[3]
2) To *believe* is to accept the validity of a claim *even though* your current understanding of the evidence does *not* compel you to do so.

With those definitions in mind, we can make an important observation: believing and knowing consist of the same decision (to accept a truth-claim), but in different contexts. Thus, when we look at Graph #2, though the evidence steadily accumulates in favor of the proposition's validity, it takes a long time for the evidence to accumulate sufficiently that it genuinely compels acceptance of the claim. For a long time, then, Esperanza could honestly claim only *belief*; it is after the evidence compels her acceptance that she could honestly say, "I know."

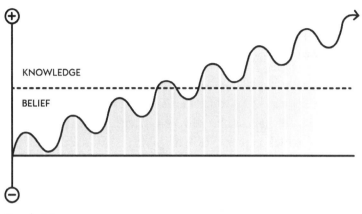

Graph #4

This all allows us to glean another fundamental insight: many committed disciples spend the majority of their lives firmly in the terrain of belief. Furthermore, believing is not spiritually or morally inferior to knowing. Indeed, to choose belief when evidence does not yet compel you requires, if anything, greater courage and discipline.

Likewise, I submit that we cannot always control the shape of our graph. Our confidence in a truth-claim may rise and fall, and those ebbs and swells may lie beyond our control. We often speak of gaining a testimony as if doing so were a singular event—as if it were a trophy we could place in a spiritual case and admire whenever it suits us. But this understanding is consistent neither with our full canon nor with our shared experience. Sometimes confidence in spiritual truth-claims falls despite all we can do. Furthermore, coming to know spiritual things is rarely a one-time experience. It requires cultivation, patience, and diligence.

After all, to whatever degree Moroni 10:3–5 suggests a lightning-strike event, further scriptures paint an entirely different picture. The extended analogy given in Alma 32 suggests a process that is nearly the opposite of what we impute onto Moroni's promise. Alma's central idea involves the painfully slow growth of a seed, and in case we miss his point, near the end of the sermon he goes to great pains to ensure we understand just what he's getting at:

> And because of your diligence and your faith and your patience with the word in nourishing it, that it may take root in you, behold, by and by ye shall pluck the fruit thereof, which is most precious, which is sweet above all that is sweet, and which is white above all that is white, yea, and pure above all that is pure; and ye shall feast upon this fruit even until ye are filled, that ye hunger not, neither shall ye thirst. Then, my brethren, ye shall reap the rewards of your faith, and your diligence, and patience, and long-suffering, waiting for the tree to bring forth fruit unto you. (Alma 32:42–43)

What could be less like a gumball machine than the growth of a mighty tree from a seed? How many of us, I wonder, find ourselves in a spiritual clearing, waiting avidly for a bolt of lightning, while mighty redwoods have silently sprouted up all around us?

By the same token, I submit that while we often unconsciously assume that the confidence of prophets and apostles rockets up and then never flags, our scriptural canon does not bear out this assumption. Consider Nephi. Perhaps because many of us grew up in Primary lustily singing, "I will go; I will do,"[4] we often reduce Nephi to little more than card stock, acting as if his confidence in spiritual things never faltered. Nephi's autobiographical writing, however, does not allow us to rest comfortably with this flattened or shallow understanding of his inner life.

Complexity weaves its way throughout Nephi's writing. Tragedy, irony, and questioning haunted him. The imagery he includes as part of his soliloquy in 2 Nephi 4 is genuinely striking in its candor. These verses do not lay out the development of his spiritual knowledge per se, but they certainly suggest a spiritual life that is anything but tidy and linear. Consider these verses: "My heart exclaimeth: O *wretched* man that I am! Yea, my heart *sorroweth* because of *my flesh*; my soul *grieveth* because of *mine iniquities*. I am *encompassed* about, because of the *temptations and the sins* which do so easily beset me" (2 Nephi 4:17–18; emphasis added). And again: "Why should my heart *weep* and my soul linger in the valley of *sorrow* . . . And why should I *yield to sin*, because of my *flesh*? Yea, why should I give way to *temptations*, that the evil one have place in my heart to *destroy* my peace and *afflict* my soul?" (vv. 26–27; emphasis added).

Even with only scant evidence on which to build our assumptions, it seems eminently fair to suggest that Nephi's spiritual confidence—particularly concerning his standing before the Lord—waxed and waned dramatically. If we feel our confidence sometimes falling precipitously, at least we can know we are in prophetic spiritual company. Indeed, it was President Harold B. Lee who famously taught, "Testimony isn't something you have today and you are going to have always. A testimony is fragile. It is as hard to hold as a moonbeam. It is something you have to recapture every day of your life."[5] We would do well to linger with this quote and let sink in all that it tells us about testimony—even that of a prophet.

None of this questions Nephi's character. In fact, that's quite my point. For most of us, our confidence in spiritual truths does not reflect only a dispassionate appraisal of facts. Rather, our confidence rises and falls on account of deeply personal joys, sorrows, helps, and harms—factors not always in our control. In some cases we can only control our response to rises and falls.

Indeed, the same Jonathan Haidt I quoted in the last chapter argues that our conscious control over what we choose to believe pales next to the power of our subconscious response to an idea. In his book *The Righteous Mind*, Haidt sets out to explore the process by which we make decisions. In doing so, he establishes that what he calls "the rationalist delusion" has been disproven.

Dr. Haidt marshals an overwhelming amount of evidence to demonstrate that we do *not* make our most important decisions by dispassionately weighing evidence. Rather, our brains are wired toward certain impulses. When we encounter something, long before we have a chance to "think" anything about it, a deep layer of our subconscious has already made a judgment about the thing, and we are much more likely to heed that judgment and follow its implications, and then subsequently produce a post hoc justification for why we did what we did. (In this context, "long before" is often measured in milliseconds, but the point is that impulse comes first, the rational explanation for the impulse after.) For this reason, Haidt says that the rational mind serves as the "press secretary" for our subconscious impulses.[6]

An example might be in order here. Let's say that you are at the park one day. You see two children eating ice cream. One child, who appears a bit older, walks over to the other and purposefully hits the younger child's elbow so his ice cream falls off his cone. Seconds later, the younger child's mother walks over and starts shouting at him for being clumsy and losing his ice cream, and then punishes him by saying he doesn't get any more. Now, if you had been sitting there watching the whole thing, you would likely feel a strong urge to jump up and run over to the mother and exclaim, "No, no, no! You don't understand! That's not fair! It wasn't his fault!"

If I came to you at that moment and asked you what you thought about what you'd just seen, you might respond, "I was furious!" If I then asked you why, you might look at me funny. You might think, *What kind of question is that!?* and then say, "Well, that just seemed really unfair." If I pressed you and asked you to explain what about it was unfair, you might respond, "Well, that's obvious. It wasn't the younger kid's fault! He was just standing there and was trying to be careful. The older kid is the one who deserved to be punished."

Haidt's point is that while all the explaining may be correct, and may even reflect your genuine feelings on the subject, it was not the *reasoning* that made you want to jump up and run to talk to the mom. You did not see the action, reason your way through a carefully articulated analysis of the pros and cons of the response, and then calmly respond that you did not like what the mom had done because of X, Y, and Z. Instead, you acted on instinct and *only later* did you articulate why.

Haidt uses an analogy to illustrate his point: our subconscious impulses are like elephants, and our rational minds are like elephant riders. Importantly, he does *not* claim that our rational minds are inoperative or powerless—in some contexts, the rider can steer the elephant. The point, however, is that before the rider even has a chance to register an opinion about an option, the elephant has already started "leaning" toward or away from it.[7]

In the context of our discussion here, the rational understanding of our faith must be understood in the context of which is the rider and which is the elephant. Specifically, we can recognize that the visceral "impulse" to believe or not precedes the rational decision to accept a truth-claim. Our spiritual elephant begins leaning, and we then must contend with that inclination as we make rational decisions to accept or reject. For many young people with whom I have spoken, it seems fair to say that their reconsideration of their relationship with the gospel consists of just that process: while they want to continue believing, they feel their elephant has begun leaning away. For many, this surprises them, and many feel unprepared and don't know what to do.

And if this reconsideration happens, then what? What should we do when our elephants lean away from the gospel? Can it make sense to stay nonetheless? If so, why? And if so, how?

All of that is to say, we may face circumstances where we feel that our testimony does not currently burn as brightly as it once did, but even so, we can choose how to proceed.

DOUBT: SCOURGE OR SPUR?

With these graphs—and the definitions of *know* and *believe*—in mind, we can also consider the definition of *doubt*. Perhaps no epistemological term causes as much consternation, contention, and misunderstanding as this one. Some thinkers believe doubt is inherently toxic, saying it excludes belief as dark does light; others believe doubt is at least belief's prerequisite and perhaps even belief's lifelong companion. For example, in a BYU devotional address titled "Stand Forever," Elder Lawrence E. Corbridge referred to "the gloom and sickening stupor of thought that pervades the swamp of doubt."[8] Conversely, in a recent essay published by the BYU College of Humanities, Carry Cropper wrote, "I would go so far as to argue that without doubt . . . it is difficult, and perhaps impossible, to feel relief and to have gratitude for Christ that leads to a real change of heart."[9] As yet another example, then-President Dieter F. Uchtdorf said in general conference in 2013: "There are few members of the church who, at one time or another, have not wrestled with serious or sensitive questions. One of the purposes of the church is to nurture and cultivate the seed of faith—even in the sometimes sandy soil of doubt and uncertainty. Faith is to hope for things which are not seen which are true."[10]

My intent here is to submit that all can be right because by *doubt* we mean many things.

To illustrate, we can consider multiple possible definitions of doubt:

The first doubt we'll call "ignorant doubt," and it simply recognizes the limits of current knowledge. As an example, a woman learning about the Book of Mormon for the first time might say, "I have a good feeling about this book, but I still harbor some doubts." Here, the woman offers no overall assessment of how likely the book is to be true. She simply admits she has much more to learn. This kind of doubt, rather than inhibiting spiritual growth, often spurs us to the kind of questions that open new spiritual horizons. This doubt doesn't really take a stance on how likely the contention in question is to be true; it simply acknowledges that much remains to be learned.

The second doubt we'll call "questioning doubt," which refers not to the existence of residual questions, but instead to the (often nascent) suspicion that the claim a person is considering is not true. For instance, a man born in the Church who grew up accepting the truth of the Book of Mormon might, in his adulthood, encounter significant material questioning the book's validity for the first time. As his curve makes its way toward negative territory, though he may still choose to believe—in that he still accepts the book's divine origins—he may begin to say things like, "I really want the Book of Mormon to be true, and I still accept it as such, but honestly I am starting to doubt." The presence of this second doubt implies the seeker is still grappling with the issue, trying to believe.

The third doubt we'll call "dizzying doubt." This type of doubt is similar to—but also different from—the second type. We might argue this third doubt is less a description of a particular intellectual posture and more a recognition of visceral emotion. This doubt describes the state of a believer's heart when the prospect of an idea's untruth really disarms him. Imagine, for a moment, a college student who has accepted the basic validity of the Church's truth-claims all his life. One night, perhaps after a particularly probing discussion in a philosophy class, the notion, *What if everything I believe is not true?* cuts through the man with sudden and disarming precision. He reels.

The fourth doubt—which differs qualitatively from those above—we'll call "visceral doubt," and it is neither an intellectual movement nor a reeling emotion. It is instead the moment when Haidt's elephant has started to turn away from a still-believing rider. This situation occurs when, even though a person's mental considerations have not changed, his impulse begins to strain the reins, pulling away from where the conscious mind still wants to go. I witnessed many young people in my ward in this position soon after the Church's 2015 policy regarding the children of gay couples. Though most of them would have said on the Sunday after the policy was announced that they still "believed in the Church," the policy struck many of them as deeply wrong on the level of subconscious impulse. Despite their conscious desires and overall intellectual attitude, their elephants were turning away.

The fifth doubt we'll call "believing doubt," and it refers not to a stage to pass through nor to an emotion or reaction, but instead to the situation in which a person has recognized that certainty is unlikely to ever arrive but nonetheless chooses to persevere in a life of believing. This kind of doubt is not morally neutral but instead is a spiritual gift. This doubt is, for many, simply the state of their souls and seems, at least during this life, to simply be the way things are. For what it's worth, my experience suggests to me that this state of being is growing *more* common, not *less*, and that it defines the spiritual center for many millennials and members of Gen Z.

You'll notice that one element unites these first five definitions of doubt: all of them suggest a state that is incomplete, evolving, or yet to arrive at its final destination. Whatever doubt means, it suggests the possibility of change in the future. Even a person who has come to *reject* a claim with what they now view to be certainty does not say, "I doubt X is true," because doubt suggests both the suspicion of falsity and also the possibility of truth. It is a funny word that way, in that the only thing we know for sure about it—whichever of the definitions we are using—is that it does not suggest something that is sure.

The sixth doubt, which we'll call "destructive doubt," rejoices in tearing down belief. This kind of doubt refers not to questions, nor even to an emotional concern, but instead to an intellectual posture wherein the person takes pleasure in destroying belief. We should pause and reflect a bit more on what this type of doubt looks like. The first five types of doubt all share something in common: a deep concern for the truth. In case #1, a seeker recognizes lingering doubts because she is devoted to discovering truth. In cases #2 through #4, the seeker's discomfort or fear stems from both a deep desire to know truth and a profound unease at the notion that what she still chooses to believe may be false. Again, though, the emotion arises because the truth matters so much to the seeker.

This sixth type of doubt, by contrast, *doesn't really care what is true*. Or, at least, the discovery of truth is secondary to tearing down others' truth-claims. This kind of doubt becomes pernicious precisely because it concerns itself not with finding light, but instead with diminishing belief in others.[11] Also, ironically, this is the one form of doubt that does *not* conform to the unifying features I suggested a few paragraphs ago. This is the only type of doubt that basks in its own certainty: the certainty that others are wrong. Our age celebrates irony so emphatically that we often elevate sarcasm above sincerity, sophistry above wisdom, and there is a paradoxical embrace of this kind of certainty masquerading as doubt. This type of doubt strikes me as deeply spiritually detrimental and fundamentally unchristian.[12]

And all of this brings us to the critical question: *Is truth the main concern of doubt?* After all, much of what we call doubt—and many versions of believing—concerns itself most with getting along with others, seeking approval, appearing smarter than those around us, or scoring points in a debate. Not all these objectives are wrong per se, but to the degree we privilege them above seeking truth, the "doubt" they inspire will not help us in our quest to grow closer to God.

So, is doubt good or bad? That too-simple question betrays itself in the asking. The value of doubt depends on context—doubting truth can place us in danger, while doubting falsity liberates us. As we search for truth, humility can soften both certainty and cynicism. Even our spiritual knowing needs humility, because whatever truth we grasp, we grasp it imperfectly. Most often, God cannot endow us with further light or truth if we remain stuck so stubbornly in our current understanding that we refuse to open ourselves to further teaching. Likewise, doubt without humility can never get us very far. When met with new questions or confronted by the fear of new doubt, we can remember that our new way of thinking remains as prone to imperfection and limitedness as did the old, and, if we do not take care, we can allow fear to deprive us of the nourishment the truth we already know offers. Just as a self-satisfied sense of knowledge can make us more likely to dismiss, ignore, and withdraw, a self-satisfied sense of doubt can make us flimsy, unmoored, and condescending. Doubt proves its worth by pledging allegiance to the epistemological quest and fealty to the divine.

In this way, our consideration of doubt foreshadows a discussion we'll enter with more depth and nuance in later chapters, but that still bears comment even at this early stage. The various impulses, experiences, and approaches we include under the umbrella of "doubt" can cut in either of two directions. On the one hand, there is a form of doubt, as we discussed in number six, that has little role but to mock, deconstruct, and destroy. But there is another kind of doubt that would seem to be a subject addressed by President Dieter Uchtdorf, who taught:

> If we stop asking questions, stop thinking, stop pondering, we can thwart the revelations of the Spirit. Remember, it was the questions young Joseph asked that opened the door for the restoration of all things. We can block the growth and knowledge our Heavenly Father intends for us. How often has the Holy Spirit tried to tell us something we needed to know but couldn't get past the massive iron gate of what we thought we already knew?[13]

What an expansive, liberating, and beautiful quote, filled with powerful verbs and forceful images: thwart, open, block, grow— and, most of all, that unforgettable phrase "the massive iron gates of what we thought we already knew."

In Doctrine and Covenants 46:13–14, the Savior explains that while knowledge of the Savior's divinity is a spiritual gift, so is *not knowing* but choosing to believe. What a beautiful and countercultural thought the Lord brings us here. We do not usually think of growing out of a spiritual gift. I would not say, "I used to have the gift of healing, but I've progressed beyond that now." So when the Lord declares not knowing its own gift, we are left to grapple with why. Perhaps it is because those who never come to know remind the rest of us of the importance of humility in our quest for knowledge. They continue questioning our perceived certainties and thus help us to learn where our imperfect grasp of eternal truth falls short of the glory of God.

4

WHY AND HOW
WE BELIEVE

Questions

- If I'm not sure the Church is true, can I choose to believe anyway?
- For what reasons might we choose to believe?
- What aspects of our belief and lived religion might prove particularly compelling?

Let's return to the story of Esperanza, our imaginary student from the last chapter. Let's imagine that she spends a few months reading the Book of Mormon and praying. After getting to know her local congregation and talking with the missionaries, she eventually decides to be baptized and, taking it very seriously, commits to all the things we as Church members take for granted as part of our religious life.

In many ways, this story is so familiar to Church members

as to sound almost like legend. In its simplicity, however, the story reminds us of this: when we speak of religious belief or knowledge, we are not talking only about an abstract intellectual exercise. At least within the restored Church, the decision to believe matters so much because belief ushers us into a world where we are asked to do and not do certain things. Religious beliefs, unlike those in many other spheres of life, lay immediate and substantive claim on our lives because a life of discipleship requires time, money, means, dedication, and even our will. When Esperanza chooses to join the Church, she is not just subscribing to some kind of Socratic club; no, she is instead choosing to pattern her life after Jesus Christ, with all the sacrifice and discipline doing so entails.

For the purposes of our discussion, let's suppose that Esperanza's path to spiritual knowledge looked like Graph #2 from the last chapter—that her ascent was incremental, even halting. Let's imagine that she weathered ebbs and swells in her spiritual confidence and that for some good amount of time she found herself firmly "believing" yet could not honestly lay claim to "know." If all of that was the case—and it is for many of us, converts or not—then the situation poses a particularly important and substantive question, one whose answer is less obvious than it seems:

Why would we choose to believe? Or, to use Alma's phrasing, *Why should we experiment upon the word?* (see Alma 32:27).

This question may initially seem hardly worth asking for one of two reasons, each at the extreme end of an important spectrum. In much of the world, choosing to believe in this scenario would come across as foolish and immature, even naive. As Church members, however, we tend toward the other end: we talk of a belief in the gospel as an unequivocal, self-apparent good.

If we look from a wider perspective, however, and if we agree that to believe is to accept a premise when evidence does not compel us to do so, then we must ask, *Is believing better than not believing?* If so, *why?* To put it even more pointedly: *If evidence compels neither belief nor disbelief, why are we to accept belief in the restored gospel—with its visions, angels, prophets, and commandments—as superior?* And then, beyond that initial decision, we would need to ask, *Why should I continue to invest the needed energy to pursue a life of devoted discipleship if I remain uncertain about the truth of the Church's most fundamental claims?*

That these questions resonate with us deeply and widely across the world is a relatively recent phenomenon. In past eras, God's existence was taken as the only plausible explanation for many phenomena that science has since demystified. Hundreds of years ago, for all but the most unusually educated, questioning the merits of believing in the existence of God would have been like questioning the merits of believing in basic addition. Today, however, in much of the world, the cultural, scientific, and religious scene has changed dramatically. In place of a universally accepted belief in God as the meta-explanation for the hows and whys of the world, the last century has seen the proliferation of sometimes militant atheism and, among many of society's elite institutions, questioning whether religion blesses or curses the world. Many people today question God, and society largely has difficulty sustaining belief in much at all.

In this context, the questions I outline above—in essence, *Why would I choose to believe?*—have gained resonance and importance. Indeed, even within our Church community I find versions of these questions coming up again and again. Many of the most thoughtful members of the YSA wards where I have worked often come back around to asking these questions in one way or another. One of them recently posed a similar set of queries by first explaining that she worried continuing a life of faith could predispose her to take truth for granted—that she thereby runs the risk of continuing in a set of beliefs only because those were the ones with which she had been born; after all, if something else were true, how would she know? At the end of her email to me, she summarized by asking, "How can we balance faith, which leads us to stick to a principle, with open inquiry, which leads us to seek new and sometimes discomfiting evidence?"

All of this reminds us of a fundamentally important aspect of belief: because it is defined by ambiguity, belief also countenances real risk. To choose to believe in the face of uncertainty, to believe without evidence compelling you to do so, is to recognize that that decision could turn out to be wrong, and to know, at least implicitly, that there could be negative consequences if that is the case. That uncertainty is what makes belief difficult but also brave. So long as we remain in the realm of belief—and we can never know for how long that will be—believing will require bravery in the face of ambiguity.

In this vein I'm reminded of a beautiful essay written many years ago by Dr. Russell Hancock, a former member of a stake presidency (and a dear friend). In it, he tells of years in his youth spent searching for spiritual certainty. Leaving on his mission, he was frustrated because he wanted desperately to "know" the truth of the gospel he was preparing to teach but recognized deep down that he did not. He first responded to his lack of knowledge by pretending to a certainty he didn't really have, but doing so ate away at him, and he felt he was not living with integrity. Finally, feeling defeated and like an imposter, he wrote to his parents, telling his mom that, because he didn't know, he should probably just come home.

Upon receiving his letter, his mother wrote back at once and said, "Enough of this nonsense! This is pure foolishness—stop this at once. Stop praying with your knees, start praying with your feet instead." Hancock goes on in the essay to describe that this letter liberated him because it released him from an imaginary cage in which he'd confined himself. He had believed until then that if he could not say "I know," then he could not, with integrity, be a good missionary. With that letter firmly in hand, he determined that "knowing" was not prerequisite to faithful missionary service and dove into the work with abandon—but without sure knowledge. Beyond his missionary labors, that letter catalyzed an epiphany that has directed the rest of his life. He writes, "So you must understand: upon reading that letter, I made a wager. *I decided to bet my entire life that the gospel was true.* From that point forward, that is what I have done and what I continue to do. I have wagered my entire life."[1]

Dr. Hancock goes on to tell how the arc of his graph has never resembled Graph #1. Rather than some initial overwhelming spiritual experience compelling his acceptance of the gospel, by living gospel precepts he has come to know, line upon line, the truth of the beliefs on which he has staked his life. It's not my place to assign a shape to his graph, but #2 seems like it might be most apropos.

Hancock's words call to mind an arresting turn of phrase by W. H. Auden that has application here. While Auden was writing more obviously about the choice to love or marry, his ideas nonetheless carry special weight when we consider the decision to believe: "The sense of danger must not disappear: / The way is certainly both short and steep, / However gradual it looks from here; / Look if you like, but you will have to leap."[2] We will of course approach the decision to follow faith thoughtfully, but for at least some of us, that thought must be followed by deciding to leap. Initially—and perhaps to some degree even now—for Hancock it was a wager: one on which he was willing to bet his life and salvation. The years since have seen Hancock become a much-beloved bishop and then counselor in the stake presidency. While I know him well enough to know that he would never compel his decision to believe on anyone—and to know that he understands that not everyone will make that decision and loves all Saints and former Saints, whatever decisions they make—I also know that his life has been greatly blessed by his wager. And that decision has subsequently blessed the lives of generations of parishioners.

And so we return to the central question: Why would someone who cannot say she honestly *knows* still choose to *believe* and to act on that belief?

I want to answer that question in two ways.

First, we need to defend the decision to believe in *anything*. In other words, we need to recognize that the choice to believe—in any way, in any religion—deserves respect and can be intellectually rigorous. This defense is necessary because many moderns find the idea of believing to be stupid, naive, or childish. It is simply not so. While anti-theists like Christopher Hitchens and Richard Dawkins dismiss believing as the play of intellectual children, William James—one of modernity's most famous philosophers—joins a host of other deep thinkers in coming to the believer's defense. He famously wrote, "Dupery for dupery, what proof is there that dupery through hope is so much worse than dupery through fear? I, for one, can see no proof; and I simply refuse obedience to the scientist's command to imitate his kind of option, in a case where my own stake is important enough to give me the right to choose my own form of risk."[3] James reminds us that while, yes, believing carries risk, so does the choice not to believe. We will discuss those risks more in a chapter to come, but suffice it to say for now that, while the sacrifices we are asked to make along the road of discipleship are explicit and can seem overwhelming, the sacrifices we make on the pathway of skepticism are every bit as real.

To William James's words, I would add those of Fiona and Terryl Givens. In *The God Who Weeps*, the Givenses discuss how our world is fashioned such that we can rationally choose either "credible conviction" or "dismissive denial." Echoing James above, they postulate that neither the decision to believe or to dismiss belief is exclusively rational. Each decision commands both our heart and our mind. In their telling, we are like Adam and Eve, faced with countervailing decisions that achieve equipoise when considered against each other. "What we choose to embrace, to be responsive to," therefore, "is the purest reflection of who we are and what we love. That is why . . . the choice to believe, is, in the final analysis, an action that is positively laden with moral significance."[4]

None of this means that those who leave the Church—or who stay but remain deeply unsettled, or who never claimed a religious affiliation to begin with—lack mettle or reason. I know people who stay in the Church and find great intellectual, emotional, and spiritual succor there; people who stay in the Church though they are deeply conflicted; and people who have left the Church after a long time trying to "make it work"—and my experience has been that *all* these people have wisdom to share and beautiful things to teach.

At the same time, however, those who have moved away from belief ought not assume that believers are motivated by convenience, ignorance, or a desire to fit in. In my current environment in the Bay Area, believing in any religion, let alone one as specific and demanding as ours, is viewed increasingly as quaint, peculiar, or even degenerate.

I am asserting here that there is nothing inherently little-minded or easy about choosing to believe. In other words, if we are to choose between pressing forward in belief or pulling back, between the secular and the sacred, we ought not assume that the choice not to believe is the "rational," "grown-up," or "responsible" one. And indeed, within our own belief system we can find ample reason to choose to believe. Perhaps the most important arguments for accepting the truth of our theology even without certainty are: first, the beauty of our expansive theology merits belief; and, second, our wards and stakes provide communities distinctively equipped to help us become better and kinder people—that is, the Church does not just teach us beliefs; it can also fashion us into better people and help us improve the world, too.

I recognize that this second reason may come across to some people as a dodge. Some might say, "Aha! You are trying to paper over the problems with intellectual integrity by telling me how beautiful the community is!"—as if the importance and beauty of gospel communities (such as wards) somehow evaded the deeper and more important questions at the heart of the matter. But that's just it: those communities spring up as an outgrowth of our believing—they *are* the heart of the matter. The two things cannot be separated. Our beliefs and our communities are different threads woven into the same tapestry and cannot be understood when divorced from one another.

My aim, then, is not to prove the superiority of the choice to believe, but rather to create a meaningful intellectual space wherein a thoughtful person can make that choice and keep her integrity and intellect intact.

OUR THEOLOGY

Theology—the study of our beliefs in and about God—is a funny thing. I, for one, quickly recognize the limits of my theological understanding. What's more, I intuitively resonate with Joseph Smith's lament about having to convey what little we do know through a "broken, scattered, and imperfect language."[5] Any theological formulation I can offer here will do little more than paint a dim, rough picture of the contours of "things as they really are" (Jacob 4:13).

Even allowing for such limitations, however, our understanding of who God is, who we are, how we relate to one another, and what God would make of us *staggers*. Surrounded by a modernity in which information travels at light speed and where we create virtual "friendships" just as fast, we nonetheless recognize, along with many modern critics, that too often the hole that gapes where the heart of modern life should be is *meaningless*. It is against this purposelessness that our theology shines most brightly. At the risk of creating a list that is overly catchy or dismissively summative, I offer here four areas where our beliefs rescue us from the meaninglessness pervasive in much of modern society: identity, adversity, empathy, and eternity.

Identity: To begin with, our theology gives us a strong sense of who we are and a deep understanding that we have come to earth for a reason. This notion stands in stark contrast to the modern world's prevailing cultural alienation. More than a hundred years ago, the eminent philosopher and scientist Bertrand Russell wrote that we humans are nothing but "accidental collocations of atoms" and forcefully asserted that we can live authentic lives only if they are built on this foundational self-recognition.[6] By the same token, one of Russell's most eloquent modern acolytes, Yuval Noah Harari, has written that organisms (including us humans) are algorithms, suggesting that our sense of agency is illusory and that any meaning we impute to ourselves is a myth.[7]

Our theological response to this train of thought could fill its own book. But for this examination, suffice it to observe that a sense of divine identity occupies a central place in the Church's cosmology. We see it in our most basic Primary song, "I Am a Child of God."[8] We see it in Moses's soaring observations from the Pearl of Great Price: though he recognized that "man is nothing," still he proclaimed, "I am a son of God, in the similitude of his Only Begotten" (Moses 1:10, 13).

This knowledge of our identity is not to be trifled with or ignored, because it provides a powerful antidote to the poison of ennui that sickens so much of modern culture. Many modern authors have asserted that the origin of much of the current political polarization is that, quite simply, we no longer know who we are and therefore turn to increasingly demagogic politics to fill in the void.

But in the gospel we can find great hope and spiritual succor in this fact: actual, physical, loving heavenly parents know us, watch over us, and have chosen to set Their hearts upon us. We look up to and admire not only a Father but also a Mother in Heaven. And all of us—men and women alike—are created in the image of God. As President Russell M. Nelson taught young people of the Church in May of 2022, few things in life can so steadily fortify us against despair and malaise as bone-deep identification as heavenly children. A sense of divine provenance could also (if understood wrongly) lead to smugness, pride, or self-satisfaction. Understood rightly, however, knowing we are children of loving heavenly parents teaches humility while simultaneously imparting great meaning to our everyday struggles and inviting us to treat all our brothers and sisters as infinite beings of divine heritage.

Adversity: Just as the restored gospel gives us an abiding sense of identity, it also imparts a meaningful understanding of the source, function, and purpose of adversity. One of the most consistently distinctive aspects of the theology restored through Joseph Smith is the dramatically different understanding Restoration scripture offers of the Fall of Eve and Adam. Whereas traditional creedal Christianity had understood the Fall as an unforeseen cosmic tragedy that both gave rise to the history of human suffering and required God's grandest backup plan, Joseph insistently taught that the fall was both preordained and noble. Indeed, we learn in 2 Nephi 2 that choosing to eat the fruit of the tree of knowledge of good and evil was not simply good but eternally consequential and critical to bringing to fruition God's plan for His children.[9]

Once we have accepted this fact, two important realizations follow. The first is that the story of Adam and Eve, especially as explained by Lehi in 2 Nephi 2, suggests that God did not introduce suffering into the world as a punishment for the choice made in Eden. Instead, suffering is somehow wound into the fabric of the universe. Suffering just *is*. But the choice to live on earth constitutes a willingness to become intimately acquainted with suffering. We learn, as described in an oft-repeated scriptural phrase, according to the flesh—meaning, apparently, that there is something about the actual lived experience of suffering that extends beyond an abstract or theoretical appreciation of what suffering means.

But our gospel's meaningful teachings about suffering do not end even there. The other point the gospel would teach here is foundational not just to our abstract theology, but also to the way we approach Christian life. The nuanced view Lehi gives of the eternal nature of suffering matters because, while it does not explain away the suffering which defines mortality, it gives context to it—suggesting that suffering is not a useless or woebegone byproduct of a terrible decision by our primordial ancestors but rather *part of the price we pay to develop a Christlike character*. Lehi teaches that good and evil constitute coeternal principles and that life's definitional question is not whether we will suffer—we all will—but how we will respond to that suffering (see 2 Nephi 2:11).

Much of the call of Christian discipleship regards our response to suffering. When we suffer, we are asked to turn to Jesus so He may consecrate that suffering for our good (see Doctrine and

Covenants 122:7–9). Note, this is not a promise that the suffering will be ended, but rather a promise that God will deepen our love and make our character more Christian because of the vicissitudes we experience. Similarly, when we see those around us suffering, our covenants—spanning from the ones we make at baptism to the ones we make in the temple—call us to bear the burdens of those whose suffering we can ease (see Alma 7:11–13; Mosiah 18:8–10).

On this point, I think it's worth pausing to offer an example from Pixar's *Inside Out*. The movie tells the story of Riley, a pre-teen girl who moves with her parents from Minnesota to San Francisco—and hates it. About a quarter of the movie shows Riley discovering her new house, going to her first day of school, and eventually becoming so frustrated that she tries to run away.

The rest of the movie, however, depicts what is going on in Riley's head. In it, five main emotions take on the form of little talkative creatures: Sadness, Joy, Disgust, Fear, and Anger. All the emotions play important roles, but the two principals are Joy and Sadness. As Riley passes through her early years, Joy almost exclusively enjoys control.

All of this takes a serious turn, however, when Riley becomes so frustrated and alienated in her new city that she steals some money from her mom's wallet and purchases a bus ticket to ride back to Minnesota. In a scene that sends shivers down any parent's spine, we see her board the bus and head toward the freeway on-ramp, while her parents, frantic with worry, call all over the neighborhood, trying to figure out where she's gone. Finally, just as the bus is about to reach the point of no return, Joy, operating inside Riley's head, recognizes that she may not have the tools to effect the right outcome and, for the first time in the movie, relinquishes control to Sadness.

When she does, two important things happen. The first:

overcome with sadness and recognizing that that's what she is feeling, Riley suddenly springs out of her seat and asks the bus driver to pull over. She then jumps down from the bus and runs home. Feeling sad allows her to get in touch with the weight of the suffering she is experiencing and thus frees her to seek comfort from those she loves. But the even more important part comes when she arrives home. As soon as she walks in the door, her parents run to her in a display that is equal parts relief and affection. Then, though, Riley looks up at them with eyes swimming in tears and says, "I know you don't want me to, but I miss home. You need me to be happy. But I want my old friends and my hockey team. I want to go home. Please don't be mad."

This moment—Riley's decision to own her sadness and her parents' reactions to it—marks the moral crux of the movie. Fairly dismissive of her sorrow up to that point, they suddenly pause, recognize the weight of her grief, and gather each other into a prolonged, cathartic, affectionate, and healing embrace. Far from dismissing her grief, they decide to *own it with her.*

With this scene, and together with 2 Nephi 2, the Pixar wizards are teaching us something fundamental about the makeup of the universe and the nature of our existence. That embrace between Riley and her parents symbolizes this truth: it is only by willingly leaning into the vulnerability created by our suffering that we can come to fully understand the necessity, power, and transformative effect of love.

This all does not make adversity easy, but it does imbue it with meaning, and it does invite us to answer the call of the world's suffering by offering to bear others' burdens—to mourn with those that mourn. And, I would argue, this scene takes on specific and poignant depth within the context of the restored gospel's teaching on the Fall, suffering, and our call to minister to and weep with each other. There are many theological and religious responses to suffering, and I am not a scholar equipped to argue restored Christianity's place in the pantheon of such responses. But my life in the Church—and my own earnest, if amateur, studying—suggest to me that our response is substantial and robust.

Divine Empathy: A call to empathy thus springs organically from our understanding of adversity and our mission to respond to it as the Savior did. Modern social-science research demonstrates that empathy among Westerners is atrophying. This decline is clear in multiple settings. A recent study revealed that entering college freshmen scored significantly lower on a standardized empathy-measuring instrument than they had ten years prior, and that a significant minority of those surveyed even feel it is acceptable to wish ill—in some cases physical harm—on political opponents for the good of the cause.[10]

Our hearts are turning cold.

In contrast, as Church members, we accept a theology that features a God who wins our affection, reverence, adulation, and emulation *not* by brute force but rather by making Himself eternally vulnerable to the pain of the human condition.[11]

Christ has willingly taken on the pains, sins, sicknesses, and suffering of our world precisely because He loves us and thus wants His empathy to be perfect. Scriptural passages like Alma 7, Doctrine and Covenants 19, and Moses 7 paint a God who very much resembles the Father from the parable of the prodigal son. When the more obviously rebellious son comes to himself and returns home, only enduring love awaits him. Not only does he not have to plead his case, not only does he not find his father angry, but he doesn't even need to knock on the door. From the description we read in Luke, it seems that even though the son has been gone for what we take to have been weeks, months, or years, when he arrives home his father is actively scanning the horizon, watching and waiting eagerly. When the father spots his son "yet a great way off," the father runs—not walks—and falls on the son's neck, showering him in kisses and affection (see Luke 15:11–32). You can feel the intensity of the father's emotions by the language we read in Luke; he is veritably trembling from love.

Though this parable comes from the New Testament and is therefore the common heritage of all Christianity, one of the plain and precious truths restored through Joseph Smith mirrors what this parable foreshadows intuitively: that God wins our affection and reverence through His love.[12] Though it was John who memorably and succinctly penned, "We love him, because he first loved us" (1 John 4:19), this foundational truth was not obvious to many Christians at the time of the Restoration. Theretofore, God had often been depicted, at worst, as fiery and vengeful and, at best, as impassable and unfeeling.

Our view of God as restored through Joseph Smith, however, is a Heavenly Father and Mother, joined in divine unity, together devoted to compassionately conferring upon each of their children as high a law and kingdom of glory as each child is willing, through that child's choices, to accept.[13] This view of the afterlife stands in stark contrast to that of much of creedal Christianity because its gravity centers not on the place (heaven or hell) but on the person. In our tradition, God's work and glory are not to purify heaven, but to bring to pass *our* immortality and eternal life (see Moses 1:39). The restored gospel's view of the afterlife centers our heavenly parents' children in it—by so doing, it dramatically recasts our beliefs about life after death. Moreover, the God of Restoration scripture is the God encountered by Enoch—the God who rains His tears on a wounded world because His children's callousness makes Him weep (see Moses 7:28–41).

We.

Are.

God's.

Everything.

Our heavenly parents' love for us is what makes God, God.

Compared to the God of much of Christian history, this understanding of our heavenly parents stuns. And what's more: we are invited—by precept and by covenant—to join God in weeping at each other's sorrow, bearing each other's burdens, and making each other's joys our own. As Elder Gerrit W. Gong has pointed out, within the context of these shared foundational covenants we come together to make "covenant communities," most poignantly in wards and families.[14]

Please understand, I do not mean to claim that our religion perfects our personal empathy. And even to whatever degree it encourages empathy, such encouragement certainly does not constitute a monopoly on this virtue. Even so, I believe the restored Church provides us with specially honed laboratories in which to live and learn from those who are very different from ourselves. In doing so, if we will let it, the Atonement of Jesus Christ can bring about a fundamental change in us that deepens our empathy and makes us more like God.

Eternity: By the same token, one of the most striking and perhaps oft-overlooked aspects of our theology is one that both thrills and startles us: we will be judged, finally, on *what we most desire*. In 1996, Elder Neal A. Maxwell gave a remarkable address in which he asserted that our eternal fate hinges on precisely this: what we want most deeply. Said he: "Therefore, what we insistently desire, over time, is what we will eventually become and what we will receive in eternity."[15]

That sobering assertion—backed by multiple scriptural references but still surprising in its direct and succinct articulation—undergirds enough of our theology that we may pass it by without too much notice. Held in contrast to declarations throughout most of creedal Christianity, however, it simply stuns. Remember that most of the Christian world as it existed when Joseph Smith organized the Church was faced with terrible, and apparently zero-sum, theological choices. Many preachers who predated Joseph taught that baptism was necessary but were consequently faced with the troubling prospect of generations of unbaptized infants being consigned to hell (or, later, limbo). Perhaps in reaction to this, later Protestant sects often questioned the need for (at least infant) baptism to avoid the twin troubling prospects mentioned above, and therefore had to accept that baptism was not so necessary after all. It seems that Christianity was faced with a troubling choice: either abandon baptism's necessity or admit to the apparent cruelty of God.

Through Joseph Smith, however, the Lord greatly enlarged the theological canvas and thus allowed both ideals to become reality—God can be both just and merciful, both perfectly consistent and perfectly forgiving. It is only as a consequence of this enormously important theological paradigm shift that Elder Maxwell was then able to teach coherently that the effects of genetics, parents, stigma, disease, mental illness, abuse, racism, poverty, classism, and on and on—while fundamentally important and even formative—will eventually be stripped away, and we will at last be judged only, and simply, on what we most desire.[16] No external stricture will be able to keep our heavenly parents' children out of those parents' outstretched arms.

Additional nuance comes to this understanding with the vision recorded in what we now call Doctrine and Covenants 76.

We sometimes undersell the grandeur of this section, talking of the three kingdoms and outer darkness as if all this vision did was move our understanding of the afterlife from a pass-fail affair to one in which we can garner As, Bs, Cs, or Fs. In fact, however, what early Saints knew as "The Vision" blows the roof off traditional conceptions of heaven and hell. This section—in the light of the rest of our afterlife theology—suggests that heaven is not a blissful and carefree reward for scoring a certain percentage on the exam we call mortality, but rather a chance to learn over the course of eternity how to love more deeply and become the kind of beings God wants us to be.

That last point—that who we become determines our eternal destiny—might at first seem to contradict Elder Maxwell's teaching about the determinative nature of our desires. What emerges from the apparent paradox, though, is something genuinely moving. Left to our own devices, we would all be doomed by a combination of eternal justice and our own imperfections, compounded by the vexations into which we are born. Because of both the expiating and empowering aspects of Jesus Christ's love, however, if we will nurture our righteous desires and give space within ourselves for Christ's grace, over time that grace will change who we are, readying us to love as God loves and become as He is, then transforming us into beings who consistently do just that.

Of necessity, that list can no more than scratch the surface of the depth and richness of doctrines restored through Joseph Smith. These four elements—identity, adversity, empathy, and eternity—deserve to be included here, however, because they stand as distinctive, current, meaningful, beautiful, and powerful.

The theology these principles represent merits belief and allegiance—a set of beliefs on which I can imagine betting my life. That choice may not be the right one for everyone—as I've acknowledged from the get-go, your experiences are not mine, and a different decision may be the right one for you—but these reasons belie the idea that a belief in restored Christianity can be dismissed as silly or childish. These ideas, and many others we could name, constitute together a meaningful corpus of succoring beliefs that can provide nourishment, hope, and a reason for believing.

OUR LIVED RELIGION

Beyond our theology, our lived Christian discipleship likewise recommends our creed and makes it worthy of belief. In an era featuring a fraying social network, increased isolation, loneliness, growing suspicion of others, and a general social malaise, the daily demands of being a Church member—and most especially our immersion in covenant Christian communities—refresh us, challenge us, and invigorate us.

Before we talk about how the Church helps us become better people by the things it asks us to do each day, we must recognize that the modern world, while dazzling in many respects, is also coming apart in some fundamental ways. To be sure, I am not embracing a doomsday narrative here: while the last number of years have witnessed some negative changes, they have also seen much good—more centering of marginalized peoples, more opportunities for the poor in many parts of the world, the magnification of previously quieted voices, the (still too-slow) ascent of the previously downtrodden. Even as we have seen increases in isolation and atomization, we have also begun to see the seeds of some new community-building within this framework.

Having said all of that, however, the fact remains that we face a world wherein isolation and atomization have reached a scale hitherto unknown. Many authors have commented on similar trends, but one particularly standout essay in this regard is Jean

Twenge's 2017 article in *The Atlantic* titled, "Have Smartphones Destroyed a Generation?"[17] In it, she outlines the startling and often frightening effects that smartphones are having on the ways millennials relate to the world and to each other. She and others admit that it is difficult to definitively establish causality here, but the links are so suggestive as to constitute a very likely connection. Ironically, while the rise of Facebook, Instagram, TikTok, and the like were supposed to usher in a more connected, integrated, and perhaps even peaceful world (if Facebook's early advertising was to be believed), the digital revolution has instead brought about an environment where millions of people, especially the young, feel increasingly envious, isolated, frustrated, and alien. Indeed, as author and MIT professor Sherry Turkle observed, we live in a time when we are all "alone together."[18] And, strikingly, a recent study showed not only that we Americans are failing to *make* community, but that an increasing percentage of us don't even *care about* community at all.[19]

This context helps provide a meaningful backdrop to explain why the more I've read and lived over the past decade, the more convinced I have become that a ward is one of the great—and often unappreciated—miracles of the restored Church. Now, before I start composing a psalm to wards, let me stipulate a couple of important reality checks. First, it is obvious, painful, and true that the people living in wards are not perfect. That may seem so obvious as to hardly bear saying, but the admission matters because those imperfections are not abstract phenomena. If you attend a ward, you or a member of your family may well spend five days in a given week at the church: YSA FHE on Monday, youth activities on Tuesday, a basketball game on Thursday, a service project on Saturday, and church on Sunday. Given that enveloping reality, a person in your ward who is ignorant, rude, self-satisfied, judgmental, gossipy, or even actively hurtful can have a genuine, deep, negative impact. I do not want to ignore this possibility.

Furthermore, there are many people for whom the constitution of the Church itself can be truly painful. I recognize, for instance, that Church culture—and to some degree doctrine—seems to revolve around the nuclear family. If an older, single woman, as one example among many, comes to church week after week and hears a talk about how a woman finds her full purpose and fulfillment in this life and the next through motherhood, that sting may be lasting and deep. By the same token, but maybe even more so, if you are queer, coming to church on Sunday can leave you feeling frustrated and alone, or even broken and unsafe. It is vital we recognize these difficulties and do everything we can to make things better. In fact, I think we've covenanted to do so (much more on this later).

In full recognition of all this, however, I still believe that wards are increasingly becoming islands of social sanity amid a rising sea of loneliness. In David Brooks's *The Second Mountain*, he argues:

> Most of all, hyper-individualism has led to a society where people live further and further apart from one another—socially, emotionally, even physically. . . . Love gives you a feeling of being grounded. Many people, even within families, don't have that. Many people in romantic relationships don't have that. A half century of emancipation has made individualism, which was the heaven for our grandparents, into our hell.[20]

Brooks goes on to describe in frightening detail the same modern social ills that have been outlined previously by social scientists, particularly Robert Putnam: America's social fabric is fraying, a decline demonstrated in statistic after statistic—everything from our likelihood to belong to community organizations to the probability we will know or have meaningful relationships with our neighbors.[21]

Amid this urgent social crisis, our wards and stakes are powerful preconstructed opportunities to band together when great cultural forces would pull us apart. Really, nothing could be so ordinary—honestly, often drab—as one of our chapels. With a few happy exceptions from older parts of Salt Lake City and other rare locales, most ward buildings are cookie-cutter affairs that offer what many would consider bland modernist architecture and make a statement about utility more than beauty. By the same token, our clergy do not have divinity degrees, and it is the notable exception to hear a rousing oration in one of our meetings. In these ways, our congregations might seem initially to offer little to recommend them.

But the funny thing about many of our congregations is this: people show up. Week after week, month after month, they come. Here is Sister Hernandez, stooped by age and shuffling into the chapel at a painfully slow pace, preceded by her walker. Here is Brother Smith, always ready with a testimony that is four minutes too long and entirely too political. Here is the bishop, a tax accountant, who couldn't compose a stirring talk to save his life. And here is the Park family, who have left approximately 1.3 tons of Cheerios on the benches over the first seven years of family life and whose children are at least as likely to deck each other during services as to learn anything very spiritual. Altogether a motley crew, but the thing is: we come.

By coming we make a community, and through that community we give a place for imperfect but meaningful refuge. This place is where babies are born, blessed, and held up in front of a cooing and adoring audience. This place is where the children sing off-key renditions of songs they may not even like—and yet all the adults beam anyway. This place is where Sister Franco, the Relief Society president, organizes endless funerals, dinners, lessons, activities, floral arrangements, and gospel lessons—all while serving as a listening ear and a shoulder to cry on for the many members of the ward. This place is where I heard of a burly weightlifter who would literally lift from her car a frail ninety-year-old woman each Sunday because she needed help into her wheelchair.

That these places and the people who make them up are imperfect should not surprise us; we are no strangers to the human condition. We are also, however, a people of covenant, and covenants bind members of our wards together. When we are baptized, we make a covenant to "to mourn with those that mourn; yea, and comfort those that stand in need of comfort" (Mosiah 18:9)—and we then implicitly renew that covenant each week when we take the sacrament. There is power in that ritual, a power strong enough that it resists even the general social fraying around us. Indeed, it can hardly surprise us in this context that when researchers at the University of Pennsylvania and Indiana University studied in great depth the social attitudes and behaviors of Church members, this was their remarkable conclusion: "Regardless of where they live, [Church members] are very generous with their time and money. Through a theology of obedience and sacrifice and a strong commitment to tithing and service, Latter-day Saints are model citizens." These same researchers concluded that Church members were the most "prosocial" members of American society.[22]

I was reminded of the special power of wards one night in 2019. An older woman—I'll call her Lettie—has been a member of my home ward for decades. She is blind and spent most of her ninety years coping with that condition in a world that cared little for making itself hospitable to those who couldn't see. Yet she persisted. As her age and that infirmity took an increasing toll on her, she was eventually confined to a group home and can now come to our meetinghouse only for very special occasions. Some friends in our ward remember and still visit her, and on that night, they had reached out to the ward and asked us all to come to a concert in honor of Lettie's ninetieth birthday. The organizers contacted some talented members of the ward who could sing and play instruments and organized a short program of sonatas and serenades. Then, they had friends of Lettie sketch her life and accomplishments. It was a brief program, like a funeral with maybe fifty of us gathered—only that in this venue the guest of honor sat beaming beside us.

While I sat and watched this all, I couldn't help but think of three haunting works of art. The first is Maynard Dixon's painting *Forgotten Man*, which I first saw in college and which hangs in the BYU Museum of Art. This painting struck me then and sticks with me now because of the juxtaposition of the heedless crowd with the man who, in his forgotten despair, has very nearly ceased to have a face. His face is just visible but is obscured by darkness, its details mostly lost. It is as if in forgetting him, the crowd has erased him. The second and third works of art are two haunting pop songs. Ben Folds wrote the first, "Fred Jones, Pt. 2," a poignant ballad that floats over a spare, repetitive, and haunting piano accompaniment. In it, Folds tells of a man who is retiring after a lifetime spent working at the same newspaper. But the day the man retires, no one even pauses to remember his life or his contributions. It is as if Mr. Jones, far from being a person, is only a cog in the newspaper's machine, expendable and immediately interchangeable. By the same token, the Beatles famously sang of Eleanor Rigby (and many like her—"all the lonely people"), who waits forlornly at a window for recognition and acceptance that never come.

These three examples—which are just three of many, many more I could cite—represent the alienation and psychic isolation that define much of modernity. In the face of these, then, how remarkable is an occasion like the one we saw on Lettie's ninetieth birthday? What person would the world have more reason to forget than a disabled, blind, nonagenarian with no local family to speak of? That she was instead remembered, honored, and very much loved is truly moving.

Our congregations are not perfect, but the best of them stubbornly stand against the tide that would wash a sense of community away.

What's more, living in congregations defined by geography forces us into close relationships with those who are sometimes (ideally) different from us: socioeconomically, racially, occupationally, politically, and otherwise. In many places, the United States has spent the last twenty-five years resegregating—numerous studies show that we tend to gather ourselves into places where we find others who look, think, and act like us.[23] It is true that our congregations have not proven entirely immune from this self-sorting. Our congregations distinguish themselves, however, because our ward boundaries often cut across racial and socioeconomic lines such that a leader may come from a "lower" socioeconomic stratum even if his parishioners are mostly wealthy or may come from a racial minority even when those in her Relief Society mostly do not. Our congregations maintain this distinction in practice because the institutional Church dictates ward and stake boundaries—a practice quite different from most other religious congregations, where believers may congregate where and with whom they please. Writer and thinker Eugene England presaged this point long before isolation had become such a national issue in his famous essay, "Why the Church Is as True as the Gospel."[24]

By the same token, the calling of local lay clergy assures we take turns filling roles of responsibility and asks us to accept our untrained near-peers as temporary leaders. We may easily lose sight of how loyally we accept as the leader of a congregation someone who is younger, poorer, or less educated than we may be. That same person, the week before, may have been leading the music in Primary or shepherding the little ones in the nursery—and yet, if that person stands up as Relief Society president and announces that she has felt inspired to have the members of the ward do A, B, and C, we are inclined to give those words an extra measure of consideration. Most of us do not follow such pronouncements thoughtlessly, but we do allow the mantle of the person's calling to catch us in the forward motion of life so that we listen and consider following their counsel.

And that brings us to a final aspect of our lived religion that provides us with an unusually weighty anchor to stabilize us amid life's raging storms: the power of covenants. The summer before I started medical school, I worked as a trail guide in southern Utah and, while there, became good friends with some real outdoor enthusiasts. They loved to rappel and "canyoneer." Canyoneering involves wearing a climbing harness to descend along a rope from the top to the bottom of a canyon. Usually, these canyoneers would descend fifty to one hundred feet at a go. Occasionally, however, they would descend a wall so tall that a single length of rope couldn't reach from the top to the bottom. When descending a three-hundred-foot wall, for example, they would descend the first 150 feet, station themselves on a narrow shelf of rock, anchor themselves to a bolt in the rock-face, pull the rope out, resecure it at the new and lower anchor, and then hook onto the rope to descend the rest of the way.

In case you didn't catch the full weight (and terror) of that image, let me spell it out. One-hundred-fifty feet above the ground, the canyoneers would pull loose the rope that had been sustaining their lives seconds before, with only a thin length of nylon cord securing them (and their lives) to the rock face in front of them.

Picture one of these outdoorspeople, suspended by that negligible length of rope, 150 feet above the canyon floor.

I've come to think of covenants rather like that. Often, when life is going smoothly, the power of covenants is less obvious, but when life gets hard, when my inclination would be to stray into dangerous paths and be lost, covenants are the force that links me to the safety of the rock that is Jesus Christ. We talk about covenants so often and so easily in the Church that we may miss their distinctive power—they become trees in our theological forest and we may lose sight of them and their power. But covenants can nudge our behavior by helping us to become like Jesus. They are constant reminders of the people we are supposed to become and the beings God wants us to be.

None of this is to suggest that our theology or our lived religion offers easy answers. Rather, they compel us to ask substantive questions: could the blessing of community constitute a reason to stay, even for those who are considering leaving for reasons that also have substance? Can we make our Church community—on both the local and the institutional level—a place where all feel equally welcomed and equally valued? If I am one of those privileged Saints who already feel comfortable in the pews, how can people like me fulfill their covenantal responsibility to make sure everyone else feels that way too? And, finally, what will it take to make us—divided, imperfect, and often proud as we are—into Zion?

PART 2

WHEN GOD STAYS SILENT

5

THE ETHICS OF FAITH

Questions

- What is "faith"?
- What are the ethics of staying in the Church if my testimony has grown much more complicated and nuanced?
- After a deep challenge to believing, can my faith ever go back to looking like it did before?

Let's return to our imaginary college student, Esperanza. As you'll remember, she accepted the gospel as a young college student after an encounter with the divine drove her to inquire about the gospel from a friend who was a Church member.

Let us further imagine that Esperanza soon comes to experience the full fruits of a faithful life. She dives into the scriptures and in them finds questions, yes, but mostly a wealth of spiritual insight. She attends her ward regularly and becomes enmeshed in her college's LDSSA (Latter-day Saint Student Association).

She goes to her bishop's house for apple pancakes on conference Sunday and, all in all, finds the Church to be a welcoming refuge and a settled spiritual home.

During her senior year, however, cracks begin to form in the foundation of her testimony. She learns about the racist comments of some early Church leaders and begins to wonder how men of God could say such things. She discovers that Church history is not as tidy and linear as she had initially understood, and she begins to question what these new complexities mean for her still-nascent faith. And then, as an ardent feminist for whom representation matters deeply, she looks around one conference Sunday at the dais she sees on television and wonders with a pain that suddenly burns like a knife, *Where are all the women?*

In all of this, she turns to scripture and to prayer, but somehow the succor she once found there seems absent. She continues to attend her meetings but feels a burgeoning sense of alienation—a growing suspicion that her moral compass may not align with what she perceives matters to the institutional Church. One weekend she attends an LDSSA campout and remembers that initial night spent under the stars. Keen to bathe again in that nocturnal glow, she waits for everyone else to fall asleep and then slips away from the campfire to find a place without light pollution—only to discover that the sky's every star is obscured by heavy gray clouds.

Alone there in the inky darkness, she can't help but feel the lightless night a metaphor for her place in the spiritual world. She finds herself in the place once described by Sister Reyna I. Aburto: "Black clouds may also form in our lives, which can blind us to God's light and even cause us to question if that light exists for us anymore."[1]

Multiple young people I've spoken with have told me stories with very similar contours. I remember well one such friend who came to speak with me when I was bishop. I'll call him Derek, and he was among the most sincere, good, and devoted young disciples I have ever known. But that night a few years ago, he came to me because his faith was faltering and he wasn't sure how to journey forward given how he felt.

It all started, he told me, a few months before the pandemic had taken hold. It was as if, while growing up and through much of college, the gospel had been to him the most beautiful music. He knew that on any hard night he could read his scriptures or say his prayers, and soon the music would come to him, calming him, healing him. But then, over the course of months, the music started to fade. He would retire to his scriptures and supplicate the Lord in prayer, but the melody became increasingly distant—like light fading from the sky after the sun has set—until finally, he could hear nothing at all. Convinced he must have made a mistake, he tried again, and again, and again. But no matter how hard he listened, no matter how much he leaned in, no matter how sincerely he tried, and no matter how much urgency and sincerity he funneled into the attempt, the music was no longer there.

It was as if God had gone suddenly silent.

What most struck me about that encounter, and several others I've had like it, was Derek's sincerity—the utterly real confusion and pain. We sometimes picture a caricature when we think of those whose faith ebbs, as if such a thing were universally attributable to apathy, sin, or bad faith. But none of those applied to Derek. His life is one of devoted rectitude. Having sat across from him during many such conversations, I can attest that he approached these questions with genuine and sustained devotion.

And Derek is far from alone—his story represents the experience of many, many young Church members. Of course, the details of such narratives vary, but what most strikes me as the thread that connects all of them is this: they sincerely want to do what is right. Of course there are those who simply fade away, and perhaps apathy or hedonism explains the drift for some. But many of these young people struggle not because they are apathetic but precisely because they care so deeply about doing what's right.

These young people usually recount a childhood and youth that felt full of spiritual substance—one where they felt cared for by wonderful youth leaders, frequented testimony meetings and youth events, had regular spiritual experiences, and seemed to have direction and velocity in life. Often, a mission serves as a sort of spiritual capstone to their first two decades of life. Many young people I know who have served missions look back on them with genuine fondness and a recognition that missions demand an unusual degree of selflessness from people who are so young, and that selflessness brought to those years a special spiritual sensitivity and a meaningful ethical depth. Under these circumstances, choosing to follow Church standards strikes many young people as manifestly worth whatever sacrifices are required, fully recognizing it isn't easy.

Often, however, upon returning from a mission, something seems to flip a switch, and that spiritual substance seems to drain away. Yes, part of this comes because of immersion in the business of everyday life. But it also seems that even when these young people make a genuine effort to deepen their spirituality, they don't find the results they've become accustomed to. It is as though the formula that had brought meaning and beauty to the spiritual side of their lives has broken, and they wonder, *Where are those spiritual experiences? Why can't I feel close to the Spirit? Where has that sense of closeness to the divine gone?*

But that's not even the extent of the worry. At the heart of the concern is this: *If I no longer feel that closeness to the Spirit, can I really keep living the gospel and attending the temple and all the rest with integrity? Is it even honest to live like a believing Church member if I'm not really sure what I believe?*

Integrity matters deeply, and that is key to their concern.

These concerns lead us to what I think is the next vital question in our exploration of the religious life. Our religious beliefs, after all, are not abstract. We do not sit around in some eternal classroom attempting to outline the correct theology just so we can pass some eternal test. We believe because belief motivates behavior. Personal belief ought eventually to determine what we do and who we are.

LIVING THE FAITH—WITH INTEGRITY

In recent conversations with many friends, I've sensed an idea that holds particular weight for many young people: gospel principles should hold sway only if a person is confident the gospel is true. If in February it seems to me less likely that the gospel is true than it did in January, then it is at least morally acceptable and maybe even morally preferable to adhere less strictly to gospel principles once that confidence has waned. The idea here is that the gospel's tenets may lay claim to our allegiance only so long as we consistently believe. This assertion at first seems harmless enough—if I no longer accept the Church's truth-claims, why should I obey the Church's teachings? But this logic is less than clear-cut. This idea may work well enough for a person whose confidence graph looks like Graph #1 (or even #2) from Chapter 3, but if we graph this notion's appearance onto Graph #3, we end up with something like Graph #5 on the following page.

While that all may seem fair enough initially, this argument ultimately leaves us intellectually intrigued but practically and spiritually unfulfilled because of this simple fact: savoring the fruits of

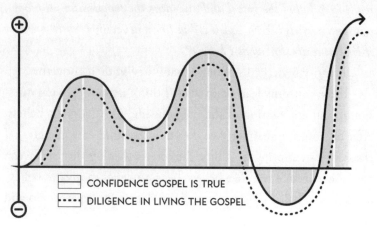

CONFIDENCE GOSPEL IS TRUE

····· DILIGENCE IN LIVING THE GOSPEL

Graph #5

devoted discipleship requires weathering the sometimes dizzying rises and falls of our confidence in the gospel's truthfulness.[2]

We would be wise not to be entirely ruled by those ebbs and swells. In *The Screwtape Letters*, C. S. Lewis's unforgettable satire in which a senior devil counsels a junior devil in the art and science of temptation, the senior devil writes of humans: "Their nearest approach to constancy, therefore, is undulation—the repeated return to a level from which they repeatedly fall back, a series of troughs and peaks."[3] If we recognize that this mercuriality is a normal part of human life," then we must also recognize that a life of sustained discipleship—to anything—will require a faithfulness of *behavior* that does not exactly mirror the ebbs and swells of our underlying confidence in spiritual truths.

I am not implying that our discipleship must be perfect; it never will be. Nor I am saying that we blithely press on forever even if all confidence in spiritual truth has disappeared. Rather, I am simply observing that loyalty and fidelity to a life of Christian discipleship will require a measured consistency that belies our inconstant mortal natures. Exactly how the interaction between those things will play out is a deeply personal matter that can be worked out only in the most private precincts of the heart, but there is an important truth contained in this counsel from Elder Jeffrey R. Holland: "Once there has been genuine illumination, beware the temptation to retreat from a good thing. If it was right when you prayed about it and trusted it and lived for it, it is right now. . . . Face your doubts. Master your fears. 'Cast not away therefore your confidence.' Stay the course and see the beauty of life unfold for you."[4]

In this light, what is most compelling about Dr. Hancock's decision to "bet [his] life" that the gospel is true (see Chapter 4) is that he did *not* actively or passively allow his behavior to mirror his confidence in the gospel's truth—he insisted on continuing to act faithfully even before his belief obviously demanded such action. This decision opened his life to a measure of meaning and spiritual depth that pure intellectual analysis never could. It is only sustained discipleship over a lifetime—a disciplined, insistent, gentle but relentless effort—that allows people to become holy.

This principle is true because the point of a gospel-centered life is not actually to dictate belief or to change behavior. It is easy enough to boil gospel life down to a list of dos and don'ts: do your ministering, go to church, attend the temple, read your scriptures, say your prayers, help the needy, pay your tithing, tell the truth, don't make fun of others, and so on. Once we get going with this kind of list—and implicitly in much of how we talk about the gospel—it is easy to uncritically assume that the gospel boils down to this. Yet President Dallin H. Oaks long ago pointed out that the gospel centers on who we *become*, not only on what we say or do. Saying and doing the right thing matter up front—we cannot wait for our natures to change before we start living as disciples live—but all those good choices are meant, eventually, to bring us into proximity to Jesus so that His grace-filled love will change our hearts.[5] King Benjamin makes this as clear as any prophet:

> For the natural man is an enemy to God, and has been from the fall of Adam, and will be, forever and ever, unless he yields to the enticings of the Holy Spirit, and putteth off the natural man and *becometh* a saint through the atonement of Christ the Lord, and becometh as a child, submissive, meek, humble, patient, full of love, willing to submit to all things which the Lord seeth fit to inflict upon him, even as a child doth submit to his father. (Mosiah 3:19; emphasis added)

King Benjamin is not talking about simply doing, but becoming.

This discussion brings us to the way in which our theology comes to bear on Jonathan Haidt's elephant analogy. Earlier we saw that Haidt argues our consciousness is like a rider on the elephant of our subconscious desires. Our elephant "leans" a given way before we even become aware we are deciding, and then we justify that decision after we've already acted. Impulse makes most decisions before consciousness even has a say. We might imagine this idea graphically like the image on the facing page.

The point is that the deeper the circle, the more fundamental the element is to who we are. That is, our words and actions are the outer reflections of our thoughts and feelings, which reflect our articulated desires, which demonstrate our subconscious impulses. By the same token, the deeper toward the core we travel, the less within our control the element in question is. I may be able to control what I say, but I am likely to encounter only horrible frustration if I try to change what I want.

But here we come to one of the restored gospel's stunning truths: Christ's Atonement can, in fact, change the deeper layers.

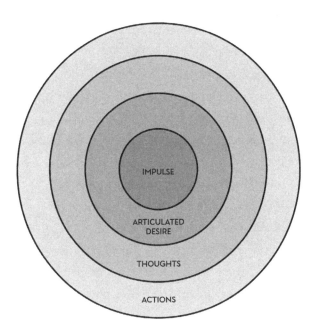

King Benjamin implies that it can alter not just what we do, but what we want and who we are.

Now, a few words about what this truth does and does not mean. Biology teaches us that some of what we want is hardwired into our psyches and even our biological brains. Elder Maxwell acknowledged multiple times that many factors—both from nature and nurture—inform who we are, at least during this life.[6] We probably shouldn't expect that such hard-wiring will change.

This recognition is particularly important with respect to sexuality. Emerging evidence suggests that sexuality's origins are complex. The search for a "gay gene" has not yielded a straightforward answer, and current scientific consensus suggests that sexuality likely derives from a complex mixture of genetics, epigenetics (how genes get turned on and off), and perhaps some effects of upbringing. Regardless of the exact spring from which sexual attraction arises, however, as Elder Holland acknowledged in "Behold Thy

Mother," a person's sexual orientation should *not* be expected to change on account of religious devotion.[7]

Nonetheless, while we should not expect anyone's sexual orientation to change, our doctrine proclaims that our *character* can: we can come not only to speak more kindly, but to actually be more kind. We can come not only to *act* as if we love, but to love more deeply. We can come not only to resemble Christians, but to be more like Jesus. The full depth of Alma's penetrating questions—"Have ye spiritually been born of God? Have ye received his image in your countenances? Have ye experienced this mighty change in your hearts?" (Alma 5:14)—here becomes evident.

As a doctor, Alma's last analogy hits home especially hard. The heart powers every other part of our physiology, and when it slows or becomes constricted, nothing else in the body works. In such situations, various medications and devices offer temporary relief, but none works as miraculously as transplanting a new heart. Such a transplant brings with it deep spiritual echoes, springing necessarily as it always does from another person's sacrifice. Still, when a transplant is successful, the patient literally receives a new heart and finds, once it is well-seated and the surgical wounds have healed, that he can run and not be weary, and walk and not faint (see Isaiah 40:31; D&C 89:20). The patient's entire physiology is renewed, as tissues that had been starved for oxygen suddenly find themselves flooded with the life-giving element. It is the very definition of a new lease on life.[8] This process is an earthly shadow of the holistic transformation that can come to disciples who patiently, consistently, and earnestly follow Christ.

Importantly, however, such change cannot happen if we are allowing our behavior to fit the rises and falls of our personal confidence curves. To be sure, becoming new beings does not require perfection—but it does require a certain relentlessness: a plodding but insistent stick-to-it-even-when-the-chips-are-down-ness.

This recognition brings to light another fundamental theological term: *faith*. Faith, as I understand it here, is the wind that keeps our discipleship aloft when our confidence falters. In other words, faith is the combination of grace, personal tenacity, and commitment that allows us to continue living as though the gospel is true even when we remain unsure. It does not always allow us to make the right decision, but it allows us to keep trying, even when we falter.[9]

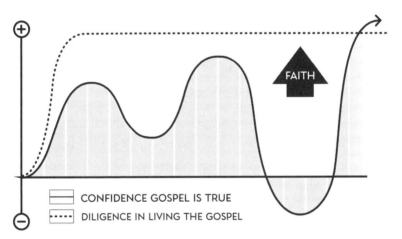

CONFIDENCE GOSPEL IS TRUE

DILIGENCE IN LIVING THE GOSPEL

Graph #6

The value of faith in this context reminds me of the writing of Josiah Royce, an early twentieth-century philosopher and contemporary of William James. In his book *The Philosophy of Loyalty*, Royce makes an argument that might sound to many of us to be anachronistic today—that loyalty has intrinsic merit. He points out that while many of us feel intuitively the value of adhering to Polonius's maxim "to thine own self be true,"[10] if we are not careful, a slavish devotion to self can make us captives to our own capricious attitudes. The ebbs and swells we discussed above can be demanding taskmasters. At the end of one passage, Royce explains, "Thus loyalty, viewed merely as a personal attitude, solves the paradox of our ordinary existence, by showing us outside of ourselves the cause which is to be served, and inside of ourselves the will which delights to do this service, and which is not thwarted but enriched and expressed in such service."[11]

The point here is simply this: we rarely accomplish anything great without loyalty bringing us through periods when we would rather give up the game and go home. Loyalty to the endeavor of becoming like Jesus is a virtue without which the Christian project is very unlikely to yield its most beautiful fruit.

CONFIDENCE WANES, EVEN FOR THE BEST OF US

I've noticed a funny trend in how we as Church members talk about the people we revere: we tend to skip over the hardest parts of their lives. I'm not exactly sure why we do so. Perhaps we think that it somehow reflects better on a person's character if we don't acknowledge, for example, times when the person has deeply questioned faith, or even the existence of God.

But in truth, virtually every believer has come face to face with the difficulty of believing. In fact, I'd go so far as to suggest that it is a defining part of discipleship. We should *expect* times when it seems God goes silent. It appears to be part of the path of discipleship—or maybe just a fact of spiritual life. This constitutes one bitterly cold day along the disciple's path; part of what Elder Maxwell once called the "wintry doctrine" of the Lord expecting of us the very things that challenge us the most.

For proof, we can look to our Church's founding prophet,

Joseph Smith. Joseph's canonical words have become so familiar to us that we may pass too easily over their pathos and depth. Perhaps nowhere do we risk this more greatly than with Doctrine and Covenants 121. By this point, Joseph Smith had spent nineteen years conversing with angels, transcribing revelations, intuiting translation, and almost incessantly interacting in some way or another with God. But in this section, he is still vexed by God's apparent absence: "O God, where art thou? And where is the pavilion that covereth thy hiding place?" (D&C 121:1). Listen to those words. Let their plain meaning sink in: part of our canonized scripture is the Restoration's founding prophet plaintively pleading, *God, why won't you answer me?*

And the list of religious giants facing existential ambiguity—but persevering anyway—doesn't end there.

Mother Teresa, one of the twentieth century's most revered religious figures, is recognized almost equally by the secular as the religious world, and for good reason. Mother Teresa founded the Missionaries of Charity in 1950 and headed their operations until shortly before her death in 1997. During those nearly fifty years, she provided care to the poor, sick, and dying in more than one hundred countries. Her mission homes focused on providing care for the sickest of the sick, including those who had HIV, tuberculosis, and leprosy. It is worth noting that, without strict measures to prevent transmission, tuberculosis can easily be passed to caregivers, while leprosy is a disfiguring condition that, without appropriate antibiotics, can quite literally lead to loss of feeling in parts of the body and eventually holes in the skin and the contraction of limbs. That is all to say: Mother Teresa's missionaries were not just talking about caring for those in need—they were down on the ground, doing whatever was needed for those who needed it most at some risk to themselves.

She said that this devotion to the poor was fired by her religious conviction, and yet it is also true that she struggled with doubt for most of her life. She wrote to a confidant, "Please pray specially for me that I may not spoil [God's] work and that Our Lord may show Himself—for there is such terrible darkness within me, as if everything was dead."[12] Again, let these words sink in, juxtaposed next to the image we have of Mother Teresa's unrelenting piousness. For Mother Teresa, too, there was a "pavilion" hiding God.

And perhaps the twentieth century's most eloquent and famous Christian apologist, C. S. Lewis, did not mince words in explaining the spiritual wasteland through which he slogged in the months after his wife's death. Lewis's relationship with Joy Gresham is chronicled in the play (later a movie) *Shadowlands*. She was a Jewish poet who met Lewis while she was visiting England with her son. They initially struck up a platonic relationship but eventually fell genuinely in love. And Lewis came to love Ms. Gresham more than he had ever imagined possible. Soon after they married, however, Joy was diagnosed with metastatic cancer that had eaten up so much of one of her main leg bones that it snapped in two. In his very brief book *A Grief Observed*, Lewis recounts with unflinching and often painful candor how his heart shattered upon Joy's death. He remembers that, before he met Joy and thus when he felt his need for God *less*, God would consistently welcome him "with open arms." Yet, in the hour of his greatest need, what did he find? "A door slammed in your face, and a sound of bolting and double bolting on the inside. After that, silence. You may as well turn away. The longer you wait, the more emphatic the silence will become. There are no lights in the windows. It might be an empty house. Was it ever inhabited? It seemed so once. And that seeming was as strong as this. What can this mean? Why is He so present a commander in our time of prosperity and so very absent a help in our time of trouble?"[13]

Beyond these modern examples lies the isolation of some of Jesus's final moments. Elder Holland says that while Jesus may have been prepared for these moments intellectually and physically, that doesn't necessarily mean He knew what was coming emotionally. And what was coming was "the paralyzing despair of divine withdrawal," prompting the Savior to cry out in terrible loneliness, "My God, my God, why hast *thou* forsaken me?" Still, this isolation was necessary. As Elder Holland points out, "For His Atonement to be infinite and eternal, He had to feel what it was like to die not only physically but spiritually, to sense what it was like to have the divine Spirit withdraw, leaving one feeling totally, abjectly, hopelessly alone."[14]

On another occasion Elder Holland likewise described the full anguish of that moment by observing, "In that most burdensome moment of all human history, with blood appearing at every pore and an anguished cry upon His lips, Christ sought Him whom He had always sought—His Father. 'Abba,' He cried, 'Papa,' or from the lips of a younger child, 'Daddy.'"[15]

Taken together, these examples constitute a meaningful pattern. We cannot know the exact personal righteousness of any of the mortals listed here—I suppose it is possible that each of them (Christ excepted) somehow precipitated the dark night of the soul through some personal choice that made them unworthy of divine companionship. Yet that argument seems preposterous: C. S. Lewis certainly did not "earn" his wife's death or the despair that followed—and in any case, we are still left with the perfect example of Jesus.

All these episodes, and the pathos-evoking passages to which they lead, signal for us at least two fundamental truths about the pathway of discipleship. First, when we find ourselves wandering through a dark night of the soul, we can rest assured that it is not new and that we are not alone. Some of Christianity's most diligent disciples have faced similar situations. In fact, the perception of divine absence may be a necessary trial for many, if not most, who ardently follow Jesus.

Second, our response in these moments of aloneness may define who we become. In some sense, all the examples above could illustrate the truth of this idea; still, Mother Teresa's story hits me with special force and power. This is in part because the sense of deep doubt was not a short season—it defined much of her adult life. More to the point, however, is that Mother Teresa responded to this doubt not by casting away the idea that God had called her to minister to the poor but instead by devoting herself tirelessly.

I think it is probably difficult for those of us who have been raised in a world where healthcare is delivered in antiseptic environments that are virtually always clean, and often even beautiful, to appreciate just how grindingly hard Mother Theresa's mission was: to care for the sick and dying in one of the poorest corners of the world. That she continued in such self-abnegation and tireless service in part as an offering to a God who often remained shadowy and obscure, is an example that challenges any easy decision we might try to make to abandon faith when our belief wavers.

A FAITH THAT CHANGES WITH US

A friend of mine took a class where she had a professor who was fond of saying, "All models are wrong, but some of them are useful." Well, now is the time to admit: the model I've provided for thinking about the swells and ebbs of believing—those graphs that I've been sharing—is limited. I admitted up front that they were very narrow in their ability to capture anything useful about the trajectory of believing, but now I'm going to admit their biggest flaw.

Those graphs make it look as though belief that has been challenged can simply spring right back to where it was before. And to some degree that is possible. If you persevere through a relatively simple challenge to your believing, you may then be able to simply move right back to where you were before that happened. But in this chapter—and especially in the next one—I mean to consider what happens when we find our faith challenged not by a mild difficulty but by something truly paradigm-shattering.

Some of us—and increasingly, I would say that "some" is becoming more like "most"—will traverse a dark night of the soul. The dark night comes in a thousand forms: grappling with the difficulties of tough historical issues, wondering where God is when a family member or friend suffers or dies, weeping because an LGBTQ loved one feels pushed out of the Church—the list goes on and on. The point here is that in each of these and in many other cases, we find our faith challenged in such a fundamental, transformative way that the challenge shakes our very spiritual foundations.

I have sat with many loved ones and friends as they have traversed these dark nights of the soul. I have watched the nobility of character and the depth of devotion to truth and integrity that defines the journey we all must make across what Elder Holland called the "battered landscape of the soul."[16] The paths these loved one have trod have varied, and their results have been disparate as well. What I want to say here without equivocation is this: whatever their path has been—and whatever yours may be—their choices do not in any measure lessen my love and admiration for them. It was Nephi, after all, who pointedly reminded his modern readers that "the keeper of the gate is the Holy One of Israel; and *he employeth no servant there*" (2 Nephi 9:41; emphasis added).

At the same time, I fear that sometimes we perpetuate the idea that leaving in such cases is the *only* option. In fairness, part of this idea comes in reaction to a problematic aspect of our own spiritual and cultural discourse—which gets at why those graphs in the previous sections represent such a problem. While I stand by the utility of those graphs as a starting place—a way of depicting an important aspect of thinking about our own spiritual progress—understood too literally, the graphs seem to suggest that deeply challenged faith should return to its previous shape after having been fundamentally challenged. Those whose faith has been deeply challenged likely hear such comments, despite all the best intentions from those they love who remain in the faith.

But here's the deeper truth: belief that has been fundamentally challenged can go in any of many subsequent directions, but it can rarely return to being what it once was. Few things are as spiritually toxic as attempting to force our faith back into its previous dimensions. Once faith bursts its initial bounds, we can never again return to being who we once were, and pretending we can will cause only manipulation, frustration, and self-harm. This is not to say that suffering and a sense of divine absence necessarily make faith worse for the wear, but only to observe that the faith will be *different on the far side of these experiences.* Indeed, what Oliver Wendell Holmes has referred to as "the simplicity on the other side of complexity" defines itself not by being inferior to the simplicity on the near side but, instead, by boasting a renewed depth, nuance, and compassion.

When we look at the examples from the last section—Joseph Smith, Mother Teresa, C. S. Lewis, and Jesus Christ—it belies reason to think that any of them would have waded through these deep challenges to their faith only to then come out on the bank at the other side and slip back into a religion that showed no mark of their having passed through those trials.

Even so, we are still presented with a challenge. Acting when we feel we "know" the Church is true provides us with a relatively easy course to follow—if the evidence compels our belief, then what other choice could we really make? But continuing to persevere in faithfulness when we believe or want to believe, but do not know, looks very different indeed. Sustained discipleship in the face of uncertainty taxes us and requires humility, tenacity, and faith. Doing just this is intellectually and morally defensible, and it can become transformative and beautiful.

Persevering through episodes of doubt matures and mellows our faith. It makes our faith more meaningful, more enduring, and more kind. Faith that has never known doubt can, if we are not careful, take on a cocksure quality that treats anyone whose faith falters as weak or unworthy. Such a blithe certainty can neglect the difficulties of life and leave us so full of our own conviction that we fail to make room for empathy.

At first, the notion of remaining actively engaged when evidence does not compel us may frighten or intimidate us—what would doing so even look like? But experience suggests that disciples who do not "know" bring gifts to our Church communities that cannot be found elsewhere. To choose to believe and to live a life of faith while lacking perfect knowledge almost necessarily brings an abiding touch of humility, a sense of life's fragility, and the need for great compassion. To not know is to acknowledge that life is complex; it is to leave room for one's own imperfections—as well as those of others.

I have found that those who do not dwell in certainty are often possessed of a degree and type of warm-hearted love that defines their walk with others. It is as if the lack of certain knowledge suggests the need for greater empathy and somehow hones our spiritual sensitivity to the pain of the marginalized. These Saints, doubting but persevering, may sense they do not fit squarely in the center of Church culture and thus become more attuned to the needs of those on the margins.

In addition, embracing uncertainty can birth a renewed willingness to reexamine questions like, "What kind of people does God need us to be?" Likewise, that lack of certainty can yield a persevering desire to become—both personally and culturally—more welcoming, humble, and kind. Indeed, certainty—a state we often laud—can become its own vice. In its malignant variation, spiritual knowledge becomes self-satisfied and arrogant. We come to presume that everything we have—personally, and as a church—is all God means us to have, and we exclude the possibility that God would give us more if only we were ready.

If we become confident that God does not wish to reveal to us any further truth, then we effectively silence Him—denying us the possibility of further revelation and effectively halting whatever further restoration the Church is meant to undergo. Our personal certainty—multiplied over and over and over again throughout the Church—becomes the bar that locks the iron gates Elder Uchtdorf discussed in a prior chapter. By opening ourselves to questions, accepting ambiguity can be for us a powerful spiritual accelerant, reminding us that certainty can stunt spiritual growth and put blinders on our ability to take in full spiritual vistas.

And that brings us to the final point.

Life often arises in the aftermath of death.

The ashes of our previous certainty may fertilize the ground from which a new, more mature, more nurturing, more compassionate and abiding faith can grow.

6

WHEN BELIEF FADES

Questions

- What can I do if I feel as though the object of my belief is gone?
- What can Mary teach us about the persistence of faith when confronted with the most overpowering challenges?

The first patient I saw die was a very elderly lady who had fallen at home and broken her hip. Her fracture would have been easy enough to fix in a younger woman, but she was over ninety. She agreed that surgery made little sense, and we soon discovered her body was not responding well to the fall. When her other organs began failing, she very reasonably decided not to pursue aggressive or invasive measures and instead to allow herself to pass peacefully.

Given all of that, her death was not shocking, but it still came as a surprise. Many deaths are painful—and some are even agonizing—but this one was neither. Her room was on the east side of the hospital, and a large window dominated the far wall. When I entered her room that morning to find she had passed, light streamed through that window, and her dead body appeared serene and even angelic.

That was the first time I "pronounced" a death, and I went through the ritual methodically. I took her then-cold hand in mine and laid my index and middle fingers over her wrist to feel for her pulse but discovered only the lack of it. I put my stethoscope to her chest—and heard only silence. I laid my fingers on her sternum and did not feel it rise or fall. Every part of her body was still. Finally, when it was clear she had given up the ghost, I recited the benediction I've adopted for my patients who die: "May flights of angels sing thee to thy rest."

In that and the many deaths I've witnessed since, the qualitative difference between a living *person* and a dead *body* has struck me. When life's spark goes out, its absence dictates not just the cessation of human physiology, but also an innate emotional and physical change in how we perceive the one who has passed.

When consciousness flees, something fundamental disappears.

MARY AT THE TOMB

Perhaps that notion is why John 20 resonates with me so deeply. For the next few pages, we'll dive into this chapter of scripture (and its accompaniments from the synoptic gospels). After we have thoroughly examined some of its most fascinating elements, we'll tie it back to our larger discussion of the life of faith. The story John tells—and especially what we learn about Mary—have much to teach us about believing.

I've often wondered, *What must it have been like to be one of Jesus's little band of faithful followers on the day after He died?* Death back then was a present and visceral element of daily life. Jesus's contemporaries could not have quarantined themselves from it as successfully as we have in the modern age. They were likely familiar with losing loved ones—the dreary finality of it—but I must nonetheless imagine that losing this spiritual leader, master teacher, and closest of friends must have come as a psychological and spiritual blow.

And that blow must have fallen with special force on Mary—about whom we read a great deal in John 20:1–8 (excerpts are quoted here):

> The first day of the week cometh Mary Magdalene early, when it was yet dark, unto the sepulchre, and seeth the stone taken away from the sepulchre. Then she runneth, and cometh to Simon Peter, and to the other disciple, whom Jesus loved, and saith unto them, They have taken away the Lord out of the sepulchre, and we know not where they have laid him. Peter therefore went forth, and that other disciple, and came to the sepulchre. So they ran both together: and the other disciple did outrun Peter, and came first to the sepulchre. And he stooping down, and looking in, saw the linen clothes lying; yet went he not in. Then cometh Simon Peter following him, and went into the sepulchre, and seeth the linen clothes lie, And the napkin, that was about his head, not lying with the linen clothes, but wrapped together in a place by itself. Then went in also that other disciple, which came first to the sepulchre, and he saw, and believed.

Mary's prominence in John's narrative is striking for multiple reasons. First, as author and professor Bonnie Bowman Thurston has pointed out, it was unusual in New Testament times for women to be considered attention-worthy—or even credible—witnesses.[1]

Indeed, when Paul lists important witnesses of Christ's Resurrection, Mary doesn't even make the list.[2] Here, however, John gives her story a place of great prominence. Carol Osiek writes, "Her unquestioned presence at both the cross and at the tomb on Easter morning . . . points up her preeminence as a disciple. At the darkest and most uncertain moments, when others had left. . . . Mary faithfully remained in Jesus' presence. This was a strong woman."[3]

Moreover, I'm struck by the intimate nature of her eventual encounter with Jesus—what Mary O'Day has called "one of the most poignant and artfully drawn scenes in all of scripture."[4] Not only is Mary of Magdala the first to see the risen Lord, but she is also the only person of whom we have record to have experienced a one-on-one encounter. It is clear from John's telling of the events preceding Jesus's appearance to Mary that John grants her special prominence and that Jesus considered her a trusted friend and beloved confidant.

Still, I'm fascinated by the ambiguity in John 20. John's account differs significantly from the accounts found in the synoptic gospels. The books of Mark and Luke both have Mary meeting a man in a white or shining robe, whereas Matthew says she met an angel. John, on the other hand, says nothing of meeting another person or being and simply has her finding the stone rolled away and then running immediately to find the disciples (of note, Joseph Smith's translation inserts an angelic encounter into the three gospels, including John's, that do not speak of a heavenly messenger).

These apparent discrepancies matter because they change the inflection of her report to the other disciples. Was she conveying heavenly news from an angelic messenger? Or was she simply reporting, as John seems to intimate, that Jesus's body had been taken away—a distressing, but not particularly miraculous, fact? Still, even in John's account, Mary eventually meets with two angels—but that visit comes *after* she has already visited and informed the other disciples. Still, even accounting for these apparent differences, it seems Mary must have experienced something remarkable, because whatever she reported to Peter and John was enough to send them running and, even by John's account, to have them approaching the tomb with apparent reverence. Regardless, what finally stands out to me most in John's account is this: when Mary finally meets Jesus—in spite of whatever sum of heavenly encounters she has had up to that moment—she still seems to have great difficulty bringing herself to believe that it is Him.

According to James Talmage's accounting in *Jesus the Christ*, by the time she meets Jesus, Mary has been reassured by at least four radiant messengers,[5]—and, of course, she has the resurrected Lord standing in front of her—and yet she cannot accept the reality of Jesus's Resurrection. It is not until the Savior speaks her name that she finally breaks down—we might imagine her sobbing—and says in apparent awe, "Rabboni," or "Master" (John 20:16).

As I reflect on this series of events, I'm torn as to how to read Mary's actions. When I read John 20—or especially when I read Elder Talmage's reconstruction and reconciliation of the four different Gospel stories—I wish that I could sit with Mary and talk with her, that I could come to know what was really in her heart that day. I have even constructed in my head and heart what such a conversation might sound like.

When I first consider this story, I want to plead with Mary, *Didn't something stir in your heart when you saw those angels? Didn't you feel the birth of some new glimmer of understanding? When you finally met Jesus—or even before you saw Him yourself—how could you not believe?*

Immediately, though, in my imaginary interview, Mary whips back a retort that stings. I can see her in front of me, and, with eyes like fire, she demands of me: *Do you have any idea what it was like? Can you possibly imagine? Here was this man, this teacher, this friend—this man I'd followed and loved, listened to, and learned from. I'd seen Him give the blind sight and lepers clear skin. He'd healed me, and I'd watched Him raise the dead.*

I'd seen Him nailed to a cross, and watched, after even most of the Apostles fled, as the blood drained slowly from His body, as His racked breaths scraped His flailed body up and down against the cross, and as His breathing finally ceased, and then I hefted His limp, lifeless form as we brought it down from the cross.

After all of that—how could I possibly believe?

Her eyes still burrow into mine, her stare unblinking: *And what should I have believed? There was no one left to do the healing. Without Jesus, what could I possibly have hoped for? Yes, yes, I felt a certain rushing in my heart when I found the angels gathered there— but what was I to make of that? All I knew was that after everything that had happened, the least we could do was bury His body properly and allow Him to rest in peace. But now even His body was gone. No, no: with all of this, how could I possibly believe?*

This imaginary interview—and the counsel of a number of loving friends—has led me to recognize that what strikes us about Mary's story is not her failure to believe but rather her baffling faithfulness *even after* she had watched Jesus die. My point here is to paint Mary as the *most faithful* of Jesus's little band of early disciples and to observe that, her faithfulness notwithstanding, belief placed upon her the very weightiest of demands. Mary was the one who relentlessly returned to the tomb. And it was she who received Jesus's first post-death ministrations. Mary's lesson to us is certainly not that we should judge her as feckless or afraid. Quite the opposite. Mary's first great lesson to us is as simple as it is important:

Sometimes, believing is hard.

But, sometimes, life's most transcendent experiences reveal themselves only to those who persist in belief through shattering periods of doubt.

And as it might have been for Mary, it may have been, too, for Peter and John. Ultimately, we cannot know just what a breathless Mary conveyed to the disciples after she visited the tomb for the first time. According to the original book of Matthew and the Joseph Smith Translation of Mark, Luke, and John, she may have told them about an encounter with an angel announcing that Jesus had risen; as mentioned above, however, John, whose account seems tenderest and most intimate of all, has Mary only reporting that the stone was rolled away and that Jesus's body had been borne she knew not where.

But whatever the details of Mary's report, what the scriptures convey was that her words stirred within Peter and John a quickening amid incomprehension. The disciples' earlier reaction to the Savior's death suggests that they did not expect or fully understand the Resurrection that was to come. Really, how could they have hoped to know—really know—anything of what would happen that morning?

But whatever they understood from the tidings Mary brought, Peter and John "ran," with the impetuous Peter springing down into the tomb first and John hanging back, as if already alert to the dawning sense that something sacred was afoot—that history was shifting on its fulcrum, right before their eyes. Who can imagine what that moment must have been like? Yes, they had seen Jesus raise Lazarus and had watched the Savior perform many other miracles. But that was different—indeed, to the point: that was *Jesus* doing the healing. But that was precisely the aspect of this miracle that would most have defied explanation or belief—their Worker of Miracles had expired before their eyes; they had watched Him take his last, ragged breaths. And now—what? Either His body had been stolen or an angel proclaimed that Jesus had "risen." But what could such an idea even mean? The very idea of resurrection was a new category of thing, like trying to imagine living stone or solid air.

The point in this recounting of the stories of Mary, Peter, and John is not to suggest any tidy or linear narrative. It is not, as we did in the early chapters of this book, to draw out graphs representing their belief or lack thereof. Instead, it is simply to acknowledge this: believing is complex. Belief and doubt battle for ascendancy in societies and in each of us. We may believe for a time and later find that belief receding. We may find the life of faith initially intuitive only to find it later taxes us greatly. It seems that, for many of us, anyway, confidence in any spiritual thing will be defined by dynamism, not constancy; by change, not consistency. There will be days when we believe despite it all, days when we don't, and days when the best we can do is hope that belief will one day reawaken.

This all brings me back to my life as a doctor and my experiences confronting death.

The *very* first time I encountered death was many years before I considered studying medicine, before taking that final pulse check of the woman at the hospital I mentioned earlier. I was a seven-year-old visiting my father's aunt, Caroline. I don't know what her illness was, but I remember being told she would die soon and that we had come to say goodbye. We entered her simple room and found her propped up on some pillows, her pale face framing a soft smile. We spoke briefly. What was a seven-year-old to say? But even then, I was amazed by how at peace she seemed, as if preparing for a trip to see a friend in the next state over. At that moment, resurrection seemed not just possible but unavoidable—indisputable—as if it would follow death as surely as dawn follows night.

At that moment, my confidence raced ahead—believing was easy.

In the intervening years, however, waking from death has become less intuitive for me. In the years since I began studying oncology, I've been a witness to multiple deaths, and at each of those I have been left to wonder what resurrection will mean. Alma says, "Even a hair of the head shall not be lost,"[6] but what can this mean for organisms who shed many hairs every day? Does resurrection mean I will have "my" body, or just "a" body? What is "my" body, anyway? Any body is constantly breaking itself down only to build itself up again. Much of the beauty and complexity of human physiology details just how a body whose cells die ceaselessly replenishes itself infinitely over decades. And after a body has decomposed, are the very atoms that composed it during life summoned back to reconstitute an immortal frame?

Clearly, I do not know. But what I do know is that sometimes belief stretches and strains us. Sometimes belief asks us to journey into realms that will tax and exhaust us, that will leave us desperate and perplexed, even angry and confused. Indeed, just as happened to Mary, Peter, and John, sometimes we will confront episodes that ask us to believe the unbelievable. In a life of discipleship, most of us will find we have days—or weeks, months, or even years—when confidence surges ahead, and other stretches when believing lags behind. Peter raced to the tomb but also held his head in his hands weeping when the cock crowed at his third denial.[7] That up-and-down brings us back to the importance of faith and the reason why faith is the force undergirding meaningful Christian discipleship. If confidence in believing were a gazelle—tirelessly bounding out ahead of us, never flagging—then perhaps faith would be unnecessary, and we would simply pin our behavior to the confidence of the moment and find it would be enough. Because belief often waxes and wanes like the phases of the moon, however, most of us will find that faith alone sustains us during the dark of night; it is the assurance that "joy cometh in the morning"[8]—even if, upon its return, it looks entirely different than what it was before.

And therein lies one of Mary's most powerful lessons. For Mary, Jesus was, as far as we can tell, the literal incarnation of the things in which she believed. In a way that is distinctive, if not unique, in history, she had seen the object of her belief broken, battered, and killed. Her experience differs from those of C. S. Lewis, Joseph Smith, and Mother Teresa because hers was not the passive absence of a theretofore reliable friend but the active, witnessed death of the person she loved and in whom she deeply believed. We can intuit a world of emotion in her plaintive utterance of "Rabboni:" the sweet release of finally accepting the reality of Jesus's Resurrection. After holding her belief at bay from the time her senses first wondered if it could be real, with that word, she finally allows herself to embrace her embodied belief's reawakening.

But the daunting lesson she offers comes in the period between Jesus's death and His Resurrection: even when she could no longer reasonably hope, even though she had no mental category within which to place the idea that Jesus might live again, *still she sought Jesus*. She kept about the business of following Him, even into His grave. She still honored Him by preparing His body for burial, even though each winding of the cloth about His limp and cold body must have renewed with terrible punctuation that He was completely, forever gone.

And yet, she never deserted Him. In the face of it all, there seems to have been some secret chamber inside of her within which she still cherished persistent belief.

LIFE AT THE ZERO HOUR

In a way, because she experienced her Master being physically taken from her, Mary could stand in her story as a proxy for those who at some point find their belief not just shaken or questioned, but seemingly gone altogether. I have spoken with enough of these good Saints to know that while each story is unique, many of them share common threads. Their shared tale matters to me: they, too, are members of the body of Christ, and their journey is my journey as well.

These people find their confidence shaken to the core. Their graphs trace different arcs but share some characteristics. In most cases, they once found succor with the Saints and spiritual nourishment from the Church's teachings. Many of them were raised in the Church by loving families and understood gospel teachings intuitively.

But then, a frightening thing happens.

For some, it occurs over months or even years, while for others it seems to happen in an instant. For some, it is a specific event—a death, an estrangement, or a betrayal; for others, it is the encountering of a specific historical or cultural facet of the Church; and for others, it is the result of a seemingly irreconcilable incongruity between their understanding of themselves and who they believe the gospel tells them to be. Whatever the time and whatever the cause, they find that whereas once their confidence soared, now it plummets, racing downward and arriving back at—or sometimes even crossing to the far side of—the zero line.

Thus Mary can also serve as the avatar for a different breed of modern questioning disciples. While it is one very difficult thing to wonder, *Why isn't God answering?*, it is quite another to conclude that God may not be there at all, and to then consider what that new reality might mean for your life and your choices. Many modern Church members, then, may identify closely with Mary on the Saturday after Jesus died. She represents the legions of people who used to believe but are now coming to grips with a universe apparently devoid of the security they felt while they were anchored to their previous believing.

For these modern Marys, once at the zero hour, they find questions cascading over them. They encounter not just temporary absence, but evidence that seems to outright contradict what they once believed. And that counterevidence threatens to tumble their world upside down.

I am reminded in this regard once again of Sister Rosemary M. Wixom's seminal address, "Returning to Faith,"[9] which is perhaps the most poignant and powerful description of this process I've heard in general conference. Sister Wixom recounts the story of a young woman who was raised in the gospel, went on a mission, married another returned missionary, and began raising children. Blessed with an inquiring mind, the young woman begins asking questions—and asks, and asks, and asks. In the course of her particular questioning, she ultimately discovers that the Church simply makes no sense to her anymore. She finds herself in crisis. Sister Wixom quotes the young woman as saying, "My testimony had become like a pile of ashes. It had all burned down. All that remained was Jesus Christ."

Saints who find themselves surrounded by the ashes of their previous believing, like Mary at the loss of her beloved Master, face a personal crisis—a moment when what had previously seemed not only clear but brightly shining now finds itself shrouded in darkness, or even evaporating into nothing at all.

We will call this moment of spiritual devastation the "zero hour."

And we should pause to describe the scene.

Arguably, there is little that could be more terrible than this moment, for in it the person looks around and finds the entire world changed. What once enveloped the believer in warmth, comfort, and light now lies cold and lifeless. The sense of free fall dizzies, and empty fear lurks beyond. The believer might at that moment channel the twentieth-century poet Hilaire Belloc, who wrote,

I hunger and I have no bread.
My gourd is empty of the wine.
Surely the footsteps of the dead
Are shuffling softly close to mine!
It darkens. I have lost the ford.
There is a change on all things made.
The rocks have evil faces, Lord,
And I am awfully afraid.[10]

What's even worse is that if the person admits all of this to anyone, she runs the risk of judgment, scorn, or even ostracization. The dark flipside of community can be clannishness. In our zeal to protect our own religious faith, I fear we have sometimes transformed such fellow travelers into pariahs at the very moment they most need our love.

As I pondered this all one night, my mind was carried with force to think of the poet and writer Emma Lou Thayne. Emma Lou, as I knew her, shone luminous in my adolescence. She lived around the corner from my parents and, though it chagrins me now to admit it, would gamely go over papers I took her, scrawling me thoughtful and detailed comments in the margins.

When Emma Lou was sixty-two, she was driving home with her son-in-law from a family camping trip when a six-pound iron crowbar careened off a semitruck, burst through the front windshield of her car, and lanced a significant portion of her face. As it happened, her son-in-law, who remained uninjured, was a plastic surgeon. As they were already close to the hospital, he rushed her there.

A litany of surgeries and long recoveries followed. It took months for Emma Lou to return to the physical activity and mental dexterity that had defined her (she lived to ninety and eventually died in hospice care from a slowly failing heart). In her final book, a "spiritual autobiography" called *The Place of Knowing*, she tells the story of her accident vividly.[11]

As I've read and reread her words, I've come to the conclusion that the immediacy of her prose as she describes the accident and its disorienting aftermath is remarkably apt in considering the traumatic consequences of a loss of faith in the restored gospel. While the poem I quote here is not about the loss of belief, per se, it nonetheless rings true to the experiences I've often heard recounted to me. Of the moment following impact, she writes:

> *Into your newly spent lifetime the blanks of bewildered*
> *   abruption.*
> *Not in on what was before you, gone the luxury of seeing,*
> *   of choice.*
> *And then:*
> *Another place, a distant light, a flower in wind, you*
> *   echoing Why?*
> *Spilled questions wrenching your temple and eye to*
> *   strenuous focus:*
> *A dark navigable by caress and whisper. A stillness.*
> *And, finally:*
> *Tangles in your head . . . surely someone else's story.*

This poem strikes me in this context, I think, because it communicates just how drastically and seemingly unalterably the accident affected Emma Lou—and this story may obliquely capture just how the "zero hour" affects those who find their spiritual lives inescapably changed by whatever events precipitate a loss of faith. What better description could I find than Emma Lou's—"the blanks of bewildered abruption"—for communicating the terrifying aimlessness that can envelop a person's life after his understanding of the gospel seems to have vanished like mist? Similarly, Emma Lou's evocations of "Spilled questions wrenching your temple and eye to strenuous focus" and nothing seeming "immediate, crucial, [or] in the least attractive," as she writes later in the poem, beautifully describe the malaise that can come after faith is lost.

Beyond all of this is the simple fact that a loss of faith can also lead to terrible distress. The discomfort differs for every erstwhile believer: for some it aches like a pain gnawing deep in the bones; for some it lances like a scalpel—sudden, immediate, and crimson; and for some it is the pain of loss, beyond physical, an existential and emotional vacuum that stretches to fill the void left by abandoned believing.

To say it "hurts" is often to terribly understate.

Our discussion now brings us back, full circle, to Mary, who endured a painful and pointed "zero hour" at the death of her Savior. For the reasons described in this chapter, she occupies a unique historical place among those who believed and followed Jesus and yet were eventually left for a time hopeless, bereft, and alone.

Yet even in the Savior's death, Mary heeded the maxim that Moroni would later summarize as "seek this Jesus."[12]

While her reaction to the angelic visitations demonstrates she did not yet fully understand, her insistence on returning to the tomb and getting the disciples to "come and see"[13] shows her dogged determination to follow the Savior—even into death, or to a confusing and empty grave. Even when hope had died, yet she believed in hope. Even when she watched the object of her faith and devotion breathe His last, and even when she buried her Master's lifeless body, and even when her mind must have declared it to be the end—some spark deep inside refused to die, a stubborn ember of persistent belief.

What followed was perhaps the sweetest reunion in all of scripture—a reunion involving both the return of her Teacher and the rising of her confidence and understanding. In this I sense that there really are blessings that can come only when we persist in making our way toward the tree of life, even and especially when the mists of darkness wrap their tendrils most tightly around us. To be sure, it is easy for us to tell ourselves this story when we experience it in retrospect and already know the end from the beginning. But that is precisely what most amazes about Mary's story: in the moment of the zero hour, it was not at all clear that Jesus ever would live again. Indeed, it must have seemed He never would. Her story, then, is one not of marching toward a known destination, but of choosing to feel her way toward the light, even when wrapped in a darkness that must have surely seemed pervasive and never-ending.

Of all the examples discussed in this book, it is Mary whose actions speak to me the most deeply. Even for believers, the dark night may come; but for those who "seek this Jesus" anyway, new life comes in the morning.

Even seemingly dead belief can live again. Just as the duration of the darkness that consumed Mary upon the death of Jesus was unknown, those of us wandering in this same darkness cannot know the end from the beginning. Yet, still, belief beckons. Faith burns brightly before us, or within us. The prospect of the Resurrection can become its own stubborn ember, the spark of hope that refuses to die.

PART 3

WHEN YOUR HEART BREAKS

7

A CHURCH BOTH LIVING AND TRUE

Questions:

- What should I make of the fact that many aspects of the Church have changed over the years?
- How can I believe in prophets even though they make mistakes?
- What does it mean for a church to be "true" and "living"?

I'd like to start this chapter by quoting a passage from author Margaret Young, a Church member and prolific, award-winning author. She was once asked by a pastor of another faith to explain what it means to be a member of The Church of Jesus Christ of Latter-day Saints. Her complete answer is a lengthy essay, but I would like to share two paragraphs that begin by imagining what it must have been like when her father blessed her and gave her a name as an infant. She writes:

As an infant, my parents' firstborn, I was taken in my father's arms and given a name and a blessing. There, I was at the center of a priesthood circle. Other men (probably my uncles, though of course I don't remember) joined Dad as he blessed me. They each put one hand under my little body and one hand on the shoulder of the person standing next to them. They literally and symbolically supported me, and joined their faith with my dad's. This circle—a prayer circle, if you will—is a common one in our community.

I suspect my father was tearful at the miracle of my tiny body, and at the responsibility I introduced. He was a student, pursuing an advanced degree, and Mom was a recent college graduate. Though poor and struggling under the rigors of academia, it was nothing new for Dad to claim priesthood authority as he blessed me, and, knowing Dad, he did this with great faith. I'm sure he blessed Mom before her hard labor began (I have watched him bless her several times before childbirth), and he would continue giving priesthood blessings to me and to my siblings throughout our lives—the most difficult one being at my brother's hospital bedside after we were told he would not survive the injuries he had sustained in an accident. That brother, Dad's namesake (Bobby), lifted his arms as high as he could when Dad walked into the ER room. Bobby was threaded and tubed to monitors and IVs, and being transfused. He said one word: "Hug." And that's it—that's the picture. Dad is maneuvering around the ganglia of wires and tubes to embrace his son, and then to bless him. It's a godly scene. It expresses the image I have of God—a corporeal being who can reach around our mortal mischief and earthbound wiring to embrace us in the fullness of His glory, no matter how damaged we are.

Young's words and specific experience are her own, but her image calls to my mind an archetypal understanding of the Church: we long for it to be a place of perfect light and complete solace, a haven and spiritual home, a place of protection and blessing and wonder.[1] We intuit that we should never face serious opposition or conflict at church because it is not just a church, but *The* Church of Jesus of Christ of Latter-day Saints—the Savior's true Church restored on the earth in these latter days.

How could it be anything but virtually perfect and perfecting?

As with most human endeavors, then, the problem for many who struggle to nourish their faith needn't even be that they have concluded the Church is bad or that it exerts a net negative influence on the world. The problem, instead, is the gap between what the Church is and what we want or need it to be—or, even more to the point, the difference between what the Church is and what it *purports* to be.

That problem brings us to the nub of nourishing faith within the context of life in the Church. That gap will always exist, and for our faith to be meaningful or durable we must learn to nurture faith—despite, or even because of, the space between real and ideal.[2] In the context of the restored gospel, the need to negotiate the imperfections of our people and our history manifests itself especially poignantly in three questions: How do we nourish faith in a Church that changes? How do we sustain faith in prophets who are also mortal men? And how do we sustain meaningful membership in a Church that is true but also living?

It is to these three questions we will now turn.

THE PARADOX OF RESTORATION
THAT NEVER ENDS

Part of what distinguishes us from most of Christianity is that a comfortable distance separates most other Christian denominations from their respective founding. The Catholic church claims to descend directly via apostolic and papal succession from the church founded two thousand years ago by Christ himself. Protestant churches originated at varying time points, but most of these lie four or five hundred years in the past. But the point is that most churches trace their lines of succession back many hundreds of years, if not a few millennia.[3]

Our church, however, is quite different in at least two ways: first, our modern founding happened relatively recently by world historical standards; and second, we claim an open canon. The temporal separation of other churches from their founders matters because it wraps the establishment of other churches in a sort of historical fog. Moreover, that same distance places the closed canon beyond the reach of modern humans.

In our church, however, we find a much more complicated case.

The very idea of accepting new scripture—of an open canon—presents us with a profound paradox. The entire existence of our religion predicates itself on our insistence that, beginning in 1820, the heavens opened, and revelation began anew. We thus accept three additional books of scripture, including multiple volumes Joseph Smith translated from ancient works and a compendium of modern revelations, many in answer to then-current problems and questions. Further, we sustain fifteen men as apostles, seers, and revelators, and many members watch general conference carefully and expectantly, awaiting direction from the Lord. Thus we do not simply believe in a momentary or even epochal reopening of the heavens nearly two hundred years ago—we believe in an eruption of the divine into our world that began then but continues in unbroken succession to today.

We all claim to know these tenets. One of our articles of faith even proclaims: "We believe that [God] will yet reveal many great and important things pertaining to the Kingdom of God" (Articles of Faith 1:9). President Dieter F. Uchtdorf powerfully noted in April 2014, "In reality, the Restoration is an ongoing process; we are living in it right now."[4] All of us alive today, then, are witnesses to the Restoration.

This all is well and good, but perhaps Church members too blithely pass by the implications of these statements. When most Christians approach their catechism (whether they call it that or not), they know what they're getting into. They may not be able to fully comprehend or articulate their beliefs, but the canon of beliefs is complete. When members of our Church attempt the same, however, we must confront the embedded paradox: *whatever we say we believe, it is not all we believe.* Nearly two hundred years after the Church was founded, we still believe that "many great and important things" are yet to come.

That anticipation adds an element of boundlessness that should reassure us while also challenging and humbling us. Historical reassurance can come when we recognize that if our religion was not what it should have been 150, 100, or even fifty years ago, that gap may be understandable at least in part because the Church of that era lacked decades of ongoing revelation. This same belief, however, brings a deep challenge, because to believe in the restored Church is to have faith in *revelation yet to come.* It is to accept that, at the very least, there is much we do not yet know about the cosmos, God, ourselves, and all the rest.

That's fair enough and probably uncontroversial. More

challenging, however, is the notion that some of what we now think we know may well be proven incomplete by revelations yet unreceived. This possibility freights us with an inherent tension in embracing our beliefs. Because we do not yet know all the contours our theology may adopt in the future, and because we must remain alive to the possibility that our understanding of gospel truths—not to mention the programs and policies of the Church—will actively change, we are left grappling with our beliefs while still needing to acknowledge that some of what we believe may be different fifty years hence. Doing so is no small matter. It requires a certain courage and flexibility that constitute weighty demands of discipleship.

Even a cursory review of our cultural and religious history reveals many meaningful issues where our Church has made lasting changes of significant impact. On polygamy, for instance, early Church members were taught the principle of plural marriage, and many of them lived it once they had emigrated to the Salt Lake Valley. While the Church legally disavowed polygamy generations ago, that disavowal can shroud from our view that many of our early Saints sacrificed much to live what they considered a divine mandate. This is not to say all did so gladly—their personal experiences with the practice spanned a wide gamut, as has been masterfully shown in historian Laurel Thatcher Ulrich's *A House Full of Females*, among other works—I am simply acknowledging that they gave up a great deal to enter polygamous marriages. And then, over the years after the issuance of Official Declaration 1, a practice that had previously been central to Latter-day Saint life became disavowed as an illegal practice.

It's easy to lose sight today of the momentous shift this overturning then represented: polygamy had not been just a peripheral part of Church membership, but an integral element of the way members understood both temporal and eternal life. It's hardly surprising that giving it up was difficult for some, or that offshoot groups still recognize polygamy as integral to their theology—they *do* because we *did*.

In a similar vein, the 1978 revelation restoring the priesthood to all worthy men and temple blessings to all worthy people overturned generations of Church policy and what many Church members at the time took to be important doctrinal explanations for the policy. It is easy in retrospect to dismiss the policy and to recognize that we do not endorse the folklore that was offered as justifying it, but to dismiss these too quickly in retrospect is to pass over the profound pain all of this caused to Black people who sought succor in the gospel family.

In another example, over the past decade, we have seen shifts in the Church's approach to some important aspects of questions surrounding the experience of LGBTQ members. When I was in college twenty years ago at BYU, the honor code still outlawed public acknowledgment of attraction to students of the same sex, and those who did so could be disciplined, even expelled. Similarly, discussion of LGBTQ issues in any form was much less common, and it was commonly believed and taught that those who wished to change their homosexual attractions to heterosexual ones could do so through therapy, prayer, and righteous desire. While it's true to say that the Church's approach to the centrality of heterosexual union has not changed, the changes on other topics related to these questions have been clear and especially important to those whose lives hinge on these answers. Because of these and other factors, we have replete evidence that, for many decades, LGBTQ Church members have found themselves at the precise intersection of an exquisitely painful constellation of cultural, religious, historical, and personal forces. They have suffered deeply for many years, and, before the last decade or so, often did so in silence.

In that light, we are brought to ask: What do we make of these changes, considering we believe in an eternal gospel? How do we nourish faith in the sustaining and unchangeable foundational doctrines of the restored gospel after candidly acknowledging a history of changes both large and small?

In part, we should take comfort in the fact that change is part of our Church and the ongoing Restoration. For me, the most notable affirmation of this came after significant changes were made to the endowment ceremony in 2019. At that time, the First Presidency issued a statement saying that while they would not discuss specific changes, "Prophets have taught that there will be no end to such adjustments [to the temple ceremonies] as directed by the Lord to his servants the prophets."[5] This declaration strikes me as surprising and profound. That the text of something as foundational to our beliefs as the endowment ceremony should not only change but that there will be "no end" to such adjustments gets at the heart of what we are here discussing.

Similarly, surely we do not believe that the phrase "many great and important things" refers only to minor or cosmetic changes to the Church. While I was as excited as the next member when we moved from home teaching to ministering, for example, I still look forward to organizational and doctrinal revelations that will make that and similar adjustments seem minor in comparison.

Still, humility will also be necessary to appreciate the sweep, grandeur, and propulsive force of continuing revelation. Though endowed with the restored gospel of Jesus Christ, even we as Church members still see through a glass darkly (see 1 Corinthians 13:12). Our understanding remains imperfect, and Zion remains a far way off, beckoning from a distant horizon. In practice and in precept, we continue our collective cultural and religious journey toward the promised land, and our explicit embrace of an open canon recognizes how far we still have to go.

As an institution and as individuals, we must collectively battle against our inclination to proclaim absolute certainty and against the temptation to tacitly believe in our cultural superiority. The doctrine of an open canon reminds us that we are to forage widely in search of truth, wherever it may be found. We must take care that a perception of our perfection does not become to us an idol, distracting our gaze from the true and living God—who has truth yet to reveal. The openness of our canon beckons us to search in just this way.

Our belief in an ongoing restoration—our hope for those "many great and important things"—can thus spur us to historical humility, drive us beyond the borders of comfortable self-assessment, and remind us that if we ever become comfortable with things as they are, it is because we have stopped hoping for the more perfect land of promise we've been foretold.

FINDING FAITH IN MORTAL PROPHETS

I have a deep spiritual witness of prophets. Indeed, while I'm not one for ranking spiritual experiences, two of my most prized have involved coming to that testimony. One occurred with respect to Joseph Smith and the First Vision and happened when I was just a kid. But it is the other that I'd like to discuss here.

When I was in my first year of medical school, I read Edward Kimball's two-volume biography of his father, Spencer W. Kimball, the twelfth President of the Church. The first volume is an affectionate yet unsparing look at his father's coming of age, young adulthood, and eventually his time spent as an Apostle. [6] Ironically, the first book was published right when Elder Kimball was ordained as President, because Edward wanted the Church to get to know his dad and it was assumed that President Kimball would not be around long enough to need to add anything more than a chapter to the end of the first book. As it turned out, President Kimball's time as prophet was long enough—and significant enough—to fill an entire second volume.[7]

The books endeared themselves to me for multiple reasons. The first was that Edward speaks candidly. In one memorable episode, for instance, after his father is called to be an Apostle, Edward shares a journal entry in which President Kimball climbs a mountain and, albeit briefly, considers that ending his life would be easier than accepting a call for which he felt hopelessly unqualified.[8] In fact, President Kimball was dogged nearly his entire life by feelings of inadequacy. In part because the book is so candid, when it recounts President Kimball's virtues, it does so with that much more power.

One night at about 2:00 a.m., I found myself on a plane headed from Salt Lake City to Philadelphia. I arrived at a section of the book that recounts many of President Kimball's health struggles. For those not aware, if we've ever had a prophet who, at least in terms of physical ailments, approximates Job, President Kimball would be the one. In the first place, his heart did not work well for much of his later life, affecting nearly every part of his functioning. In addition, he once had half of his face paralyzed, and at one time he developed a blistering skin condition that left him covered in boils. Even further, and perhaps most famously, he developed throat cancer and had to have virtually his entire voice box surgically removed, leaving him with the bullfrog voice many older members remember.

The section of the book I was reading that night recounts the story of a time when President Kimball visited an area conference in Central America. As he sat on the dais while the meeting worked its way through, he leaned over to the local authorities accompanying him and said, "I would like to meet the people." This request was likely to cause problems for multiple reasons. First, President Kimball was quite elderly by that time, and his heart was already failing—and the conference occurred at around six thousand feet above sea level. Moreover, this conference took place in a sports stadium with thousands in attendance. The other leaders there guessed that if they announced President Kimball would be greeting people, there would be a rush to the front. After a couple of inquiries about making it work, however, and over the protests of Elder Bruce R. McConkie and President Kimball's private physician, the others finally relented to President Kimball's intonation that "if you saw these people as I do, you would not try to keep me from greeting them." Forming an informal greeting line once the meeting ended, the leaders made it known that the prophet would greet anyone who wanted to come to the front. There was a momentary crush as had been feared, but once the crowd saw President Kimball was not going anywhere, they formed a quiet and orderly line, and he stayed to shake the hand of—and often embrace—*every single person* who wished to come.

I will never forget the night I read this story by the pale light of that red-eye flight on the way to Philadelphia. At one point, that *thing* I described back in Chapter 3 as happening to Esperanza happened to me. I am not one for crying, but, as I read, I found myself overcome by the sense that this was a holy act from a prophet of God. I felt bathed in light, aglow with serenity and spiritual confidence.

Alongside this holy moment from that plane ride to Philadelphia are nestled a host of other experiences that fortify my trust in and testimony of modern prophets. As I have set out to learn from their words and examples, by far what has most impressed me is their genuine conviction and their deep-seated desire to bring others to Christ. Still, even while I am nourished by these many episodes, there still sit next to them occurrences, facts, and quotes from modern prophets that leave me puzzled, concerned, and sometimes, frankly, brokenhearted. I want to mention some of these difficult issues here; thereafter, we will consider what all this means.

I think here of reading lifelong Church member Richard Bushman's biography of Joseph Smith, *Rough Stone Rolling,* and learning for the first time that Joseph had married many women, that some of those women were only teenagers, that some of the women were already married to other men, that most of the marriages were at least initially hidden from Emma, and that at least some of the marriages appear to have been physically consummated (though evidence suggests that was at least mostly not the case with sealings to married women, and that Joseph never fathered a child with any of his polygamous wives). Because these relationships were conducted in such privacy, much remains unknown about them. Even so, just the rough outline, at least on its surface, seems deeply troubling.[9]

By the same token, my heart has been broken to learn that, while the historical record indicates that Joseph Smith preached a gospel of near-universal inclusion, his successors changed Church policy to exclude those of African descent from entering our temples or, in the case of men, from holding the priesthood. I have been disheartened to read the way in which Brigham Young and other contemporary leaders discussed those of African descent.

Indeed, for more than one hundred years after the institution of the racial exclusion policy, both formal and informal actions made the Church too often hostile to people of African descent.

Because all this was true, the revelation of 1978 was not a new policy but instead a *restoration* of the policy Joseph Smith had initially implemented.[10]

More recently, I've learned with a heavy heart more about the way some of our modern prophets have addressed LGBTQ members of our faith and queer sexual and gender orientation in general. As has been well documented, for example, in the 1970s and 1980s, prophets and apostles generally taught that sexuality was mutable and that gay people could become straight through religious devotion. Even in more recent years, this belief has been perpetuated from the pulpit. And, until the last decade, public acknowledgment of homosexual attraction was considered a serious honor code violation at Church schools. These teachings caused deep, lasting pain to many of our queer members—and, while many of these specifics have now been changed or abandoned, even in 2023, many queer members continue to struggle mightily to find acceptance, love, and belonging in the Church. The landscape has changed, but real, deep, and piercing pain remains.

I bring these things up not to point fingers but rather because they represent places where our prophets previously taught things the Church no longer teaches. President Russell M. Nelson and President Dallin H. Oaks, for example, have recently come out forcefully and repeatedly against racism, with President Nelson telling the general Church membership that we must "lead out in abandoning attitudes and actions of prejudice"[11] and with President Oaks declaring at a BYU devotional that the phrase "Black lives matters" is an "eternal truth" with unassailable doctrinal foundations.[12] By the same token, the Church has, in recent years, added a great deal of nuance in our dealings with members of the LGBTQ community—with President M. Russell Ballard stating in 2017, "We need to listen and understand what our LGBT brothers and sisters are experiencing. Certainly we must do better than we have done in the past."[13] Without dismissing or diminishing the pain and confusion that many queer members and their families still feel, we can nonetheless recognize that the Church no longer teaches that sexuality is mutable, has specifically denounced conversion therapy, has encouraged members to approach our brothers and sisters with charity regardless of their sexuality or gender orientation, and has made institutional attempts to find areas of agreement and compromise with LGBTQ civil rights groups even in places where doctrines and policies remain unchanged.

It's one thing to note that these teachings have changed, but the larger point here is to acknowledge that some Church teachings from previous eras were wrong and harmful—a truth we can now recognize precisely because those old teachings have been *superseded by greater light and further revelation.* This recognition is implicit in President Uchtdorf's 2013 teaching in general conference:

> To be perfectly frank, there have been times when members or leaders in the church have simply made mistakes. There may have been things said or done that were not in harmony with our values, principles, or doctrine. I suppose the church would be perfect only if it were run by perfect beings. God is perfect, and His doctrine is pure. But He works through us—his imperfect children—and imperfect people make mistakes.[14]

All to say: today we can recognize the mistakes of the past—and with that recognition, the Church has disavowed some policies, practices, and teachings that were once commonly accepted. We as Church members need to grapple with this. The racist rhetoric of past Church members and leaders, for example, made—and make—the gospel family an inhospitable home for many members of color. Similarly, many queer Church members have recounted that the teaching that homosexuality could and should be changed into heterosexuality—trying to find peace by becoming straight through increased religious devotion—led them to a place of isolation and despair.

This all became more real to me when I began serving in a YSA bishopric several years ago and spent many hours counseling with a young man who had attended BYU years before. He described his anguish in trying—again, and again, and again—to achieve a transformation of his sexuality, only to find that the homosexuality simply would not change. So desperate was his despair that he used to think frequently of suicide. I cannot adequately describe the anguish and heartache I felt on this young man's behalf. My heart beat and broke in harmony with his.

And this brings us to a central seeming contradiction at the heart of life in the restored Church. For many people, being a member of the Church is definitionally hard. Black members, queer members, poor members, women—all of these, and many more, may feel acutely the sting of marginalized membership in ways those who do not belong to these groups simply can never understand. Yet, it is also true that the Church teaches powerful and nourishing doctrines that offer comfort in an era of fear and purpose in an age that often feels meaningless. Similarly, Church communities—and the covenants the bind us to God and to each other—really can provide a place of acceptance and enveloping love that stands in bright contrast to a world that too often languishes in loneliness, apathy, and hatred.

Therein lies a foundational paradox—one we need to sit with and consider. This paradox challenges our notions of modern prophets precisely because their words are so central to the way we as members construct Church life and our own lives. The words prophets say matter precisely because we invest them with such gravity and importance. Our attempts to follow prophetic counsel are a large part of what make the Church what it is.

In light of the apparent contradiction, it would be easy to abandon one side of the paradox. "Well," we might say, "the pain of those marginalized Church members must not be real. They just need to 'buck up' or to start living the gospel more fully." Or, on the other hand, we might say to ourselves, "Oh well, the Church never really meant much to me anyway. The doctrines hold no power. The community is not that remarkable. There was never anything really there."

The longer I live, however, the more convinced I become of this truth: we discover life's most meaningful lessons by leaning into, not away from, paradox. Thus, when confronted with these twin realities, we must lean into the apparent contradiction.

We must find what truth and grace we can there.

Now, to be clear: this active "leaning in" may not be right for every person at every moment along the journey. The paradox I am discussing here can be genuinely painful for some members and, if that's the case for you, you may wish to take time for yourself before that leaning in.

For those who wish to more squarely confront this paradox, however, we are helped in leaning in by reading pleas from prophets themselves, especially in the Book of Mormon. Listen—no, really, listen—to this message from Nephi (I'm going to paraphrase 2 Nephi 33:3–4 in a way I consider faithful to his intent, hoping to update the vernacular a bit to make it more accessible and immediate):

> *I, Nephi, have written what I have written, and I think*
> *it's pretty good, especially for my descendants. I think about*
> *them all the time and pray for them every night. I pray to God*
> *for them—that my words will help them—and I trust God*

will hear my cry. But I also recognize that my words are weak,
and I am imperfect. When I say I trust God I mean that I trust
He will take the things I've written—as imperfect as they may
be—and make them what I alone cannot. If all else fails, please
recognize that I've written what I've written to bring people to
Christ—if I somehow mess this up, I hope you'll look to Him,
and not to me.

So, there we have the closing message of the book's first author.
Then, as Moroni is wrapping up the translation of the Jaredite record, we hear words of striking similarity. He has just explained how
he was commanded by the Lord to write this record, and then continues (again, I paraphrase for effect from Ether 12:23–25):

> *I responded to the Lord, "Lord, the people who read this*
> *will not be impressed. If only I could write powerfully, like the*
> *brother of Jared. I'll even admit that when I get up and give*
> *a speech, the Spirit carries my intent to the heart of my listen-*
> *ers. But when I write—it's just a mess. I'm awkward. Nothing*
> *comes across as I mean it. When I write, I recognize just how*
> *weak I really am, and I am left frightened that my weak writ-*
> *ing will not be sufficient to deliver the power and majesty of the*
> *message I've been commanded to convey."*

So, here is the overwhelmingly important message that both
Nephi and Moroni bring: prophets recognize that, as mortal men,
they are unequal to the mantle placed upon their backs. Saying so
is not sacrilege; it is mortal reality. As Elder Jeffrey R. Holland aptly
put it, "Imperfect people are all God has ever had to work with.
That must be terribly frustrating to Him, but He deals with it. So
should we."[15]

Just after the string of verses paraphrased above, Moroni
teaches us an important truth about what he thought about himself
as a prophet, and how we can approach a church where prophets

WHEN CHURCH IS HARD

lead us. He writes: "And when I had said this, the Lord spake unto me, saying: Fools mock, but they shall mourn" (Ether 12:26). Now, let's pause for a moment, because up to this point it may sound as if the Lord is simply rebuking those who acknowledge the imperfections of the Lord's servants. But Moroni rescues us from this misreading by writing: "And my grace is sufficient for the meek, that they shall take no advantage of your weakness" (v. 26). And then, in words many of us memorized in seminary, "And if men come unto me I will show unto them their weakness. I give unto men weakness that they may be humble; and my grace is sufficient for all men that humble themselves before me" (v. 27).

Those verses do not constitute an invitation to turn a blind eye to the shortcomings of Nephi, Moroni, or any modern prophet. But neither do they justify dismissing their prophetic roles. These verses, understood in context, suggest to me that when we feel we or those we love have been hurt by the teachings, words, or actions of a Church leader, we must then do what we do when we encounter suffering in any arena of human endeavor: we seek grace and healing from Jesus. We can acknowledge the reality of hurt while still seeking to understand the truths prophets would teach us by the light of Jesus's love.

The gospel of Christ, rich in paradox, is a realm of "and," not a kingdom of "or."

Indeed, this teaching seems to be at the heart of one of the Book of Mormon's most stirring verses. As best we can tell, when Moroni wrote Mormon chapter 9, he thought he was bidding his future readers farewell (he was later surprised to have the time and wherewithal to be able to write the book of Moroni). We need to remember that he is not closing just his own book but believes he is also closing the books of all the accumulated prophets that he and his father have compiled into this record. What a weight he carries as he prepares to say goodbye. And so, etching these words into metal plates, believing he will never have another chance to address his future audience, what does he choose to write?

> Condemn me not because of mine imperfection, neither my father, because of his imperfection, neither them who have written before him; but rather give thanks unto God that he hath made manifest unto you our imperfections, that ye may learn to be more wise than we have been. (Mormon 9:31)

This verse is stunning—especially coming, as it does, as a sort of benediction that he apparently thought would help to close the entire prophetic compendium. Who, more than Moroni and Mormon, would have been more painfully aware not only of their own prophetic shortcomings but also of those of all the prophets who preceded them? It can hardly surprise us—and yet it does—that Moroni here writes with such grace and patience, such wisdom and insight. And this invitation conveys a faith-changing paradox. Not only is it not wrong to appropriately identify prophetic "imperfection," but doing so should, by prophetic direction, be cause for us to thank God—and to allow Christ's grace to lead us to grow in wisdom and godly love.

The process of grappling with prophetic imperfection is one with which the Book of Mormon's authors were well familiar. We should not be surprised when this same demand of discipleship also weighs on us.

Our recognizing prophetic fallibility, then, becomes an invitation to recognize that all of us—deacons and prophets, Primary teachers and Relief Society presidents, young and old, "black and white, bond and free, male and female" (2 Nephi 26:33)—are imperfect beings desperately in need of the saving grace of Jesus. We are all, as King Benjamin so succinctly reminds us, "beggars"

(Mosiah 4:19). The imperfections of prophets must therefore draw us back to the necessity of the Atonement, grace, and love of Jesus Christ. We must awaken to the universality of that need—to the deep, aching pain that only divine intervention can salve. Indeed, as Moroni surveys the story of the brother of Jared, the twin disintegrations of the Nephite and Jaredite societies, and the weight of his own weakness, is it any wonder that he closes the benedictory chapter 12 of Ether with this plaintive plea?

> And then shall ye know that I have seen Jesus, and that he hath talked with me face to face, and that he told me in plain humility, even as a man telleth another in mine own language, concerning these things; And only a few have I written, because of my weakness in writing. And now, *I would commend you to seek this Jesus* of whom the prophets and apostles have written, that the grace of God the Father, and also the Lord Jesus Christ, and the Holy Ghost, which beareth record of them, may be and abide in you forever. Amen. (Ether 12:39–41; emphasis added)

We must allow prophets, even in their self-acknowledged weakness, to draw us toward the Savior—to do otherwise is to look beyond the mark because, as Elder Neal A. Maxwell said, "The mark is Christ."[16]

THE CHURCH IS A BUILDING, BUT ALSO A BODY

It is usually at about this point in the dialogue that someone will interject, "But if all you say here is true, then how is our church any different from any other church? If our church has stuff it 'got wrong' in the past, then how does it differ from any organization led by decent folks who are just trying to do what's right?"

There is no easy answer here, but we might begin by

questioning some of the assumptions that underlie the questions themselves.

When I was a missionary trying to explain the Restoration, we would often use plastic cups to suggest that the Church had been built on four foundations: prophets, priesthood, revelation, and scripture. Questions about whether those four pillars are the correct ones aside (where, for example, is the Atonement of Jesus Christ in this example?), what most strikes me about this simple object lesson is the idea that "the Church" is a staid, concrete thing that can be constructed like a building. This assumption suggests that "the Church" consists of certain unalterable elements and that, once those have been restored, the Church is whole and complete—no more construction needed.

If we understand the Restoration of the Church in this way, it follows that we would be left with a bevy of uncomfortable questions if the Church ever evolved. Buildings, after all, don't generally change in any significant or fundamental way—they simply are what they are. And in some ways this is true of the Church. There are some foundational aspects of our religion that represent its unmoving foundations and may never change. All to say: in some ways, the Church is very much a building. Still, if the Church were only like a building, we could fairly expect that the architect would have built it as it should have been from the get-go so that it could then stand forever, like a cathedral, deepening in legend, sentiment, and beauty over time, but never changing foundationally.

While understanding the Church as a building can help us to think about its nature and function, this analogy remains incomplete. We need to move beyond it to fully grasp what the Church is and what it is meant to do in our lives. In this vein, we turn to Paul's formulation that we belong not to the building, but to the *body* of the Church. We are not only windows and doors and steeples of Christ's Church but, instead, eyes, neurons, and hearts (see 1 Corinthians 12). This metaphor offers us additional insight as we seek to understand the Church and its evolution over time— but it also lays a challenge at our feet.

If, as Christ assures us in the opening section of the Doctrine and Covenants, The Church of Jesus Christ of Latter-day Saints is "the only true and living church" (D&C 1:30), perhaps we can spend more time and energy focusing on what it means for a church to live. This two-adjective description seems calculated *against* allowing us to conceptualize the Church as a fixed thing Joseph Smith built and to which subsequent prophets have occasionally added ornamental moldings. Instead, within a living Church, we must all see ourselves as meaningful, active, organically connected members. Just as any real body makes its way through life via biological processes that are defined by both genetic and psychological evolution, perhaps we ought not be surprised at— and indeed should lean into—the changes that come to the Church over time.

This all brings us back to those insistent questions: *If living means evolving, how can the Church be both true and evolving? If the Church changes its stance on important issues, then what makes it any truer than any other church or well-meaning organization?*

Some parts of the answer to this question can be understood only within the most private chambers of an individual seeker's heart. What I offer as a beginning of an answer here, however, echoes themes I have already explored in previous chapters. What I think most makes the living Church true is:

1) a soaring theology distinguished by sometimes subtle and sometimes radical departures from creedal Christianity and that, when taken in its entirety, offers

a grand and robust set of answers to modernity's most pressing existential questions;

2) covenant communities where we strive to become like Jesus while lifting and building the Saints who surround us;

3) access to unique authority, because of the restoration of the priesthood and restored priesthood keys, that underlies both apostolic witness and everyday gospel ordinances, buttressing everything from the baptism that rebirths new members as covenant disciples to the final welding together of the whole human family; and,

4) an environment, a set of precepts, and access to the power of grace that transform us into men and women of Christ.

Understood in that way, we approach a fundamental truth about the restored gospel. Perhaps we are initially kept from it because we mistakenly sit with my missionary self, visualizing the Church *only* as a building to be built. To be clear, my point here is not that the building metaphor is not powerful, useful, or helpful. As stated earlier, there are some ways in which the Church is like a building, with Christ as the chief cornerstone. This unchanging foundation is the very thing that protects the Church from being a feather to every societal wind and that ensures the Church is protected as explained in Helaman 5:12.

Still, we cannot think of the Church as *only* a building. Doing so misses a fundamental point. What if—at least as much as it is a building—the Church is a body that is made of all of us? And what if, as in the human body, the magic comes not with this isolated finger or with that nerve alone, but instead by the physiologic symphony evident only when neuron speaks to neuron, by the reciprocity between heart and lungs, by the cellular differences that make a kidney different from a liver and both very different from the brain? And what if, as with any human body, the full beauty of a being comes not in the magical innocence of childhood but as the Church ages, grows, and gets closer to measuring up to the stature of the fullness of Christ?

What if the magic of the Church comes in the fact that the institutional Church gives both the authority to carry out necessary ordinances as well as the space and time for individual members to learn to work together—such that its evolution becomes not a force of which we should be frightened but, as in real biology, the elemental drive pushing the Church's "physiology" ever closer to perfection?

In my mind, these are some of the most important ways that the Church helps us become like Jesus. The Church's evolution need not frighten us, because it is the very hallmark of Christ's Church: His true Church is the organizational and logistical distillation of a people, bound together by covenant and brought into proximity by weekly worship, working our imperfect way toward Zion. That very struggle—one in which we endlessly come up against our own flaws and even the flaws of those who lead us—defines the true and living Church. And it is partly for this reason that the Church we believe in will never have "been restored," but is instead forever in the process of restoration.

This process continues only as we join together in consecrating our gifts for the building up of Zion. And it is in this context that we come to understand the importance of spiritual gifts, a concept so central to the restored gospel we find it outlined by Paul in 1 Corinthians 12, by Moroni in the Book of Mormon's last chapter, and by the Lord Himself in a revelation to Joseph Smith now recorded as Doctrine and Covenants 46. The Lord's prophets seem determined to drive into us just how much spiritual gifts matter. But why?

To answer this, let's begin by reading from Doctrine and Covenants 46:8–12:

> Seek ye earnestly the best gifts, always remembering for what they are given; For verily I say unto you, they are given for the benefit of those who love me and keep all my commandments, and him that seeketh so to do; that all may be benefited that seek or that ask of me . . . And again, verily I say unto you, I would that ye should always remember, and always retain in your minds what those gifts are, that are given unto the church. For all have not every gift given unto them; for there are many gifts, and to every man is given a gift by the Spirit of God. To some is given one, and to some is given another, that all may be profited thereby.

It is as if we are created purposefully incomplete. To Paul's point about being members of the body of Christ—each of us does certain things well but lacks in other areas, and thus it is only by banding together in families and wards that we become complete Christian organisms. Brother Santos blesses the ward by keeping punctilious records; Sister Beckham by playing the organ; Brother Freeman by sincerely complimenting everyone he meets; Sister Hernandez by how she—and only she—can really teach the Sunbeams; Brother Frank by ministering as bishop; Sister Francois by leading as Relief Society President; Brother Lim by teaching Sunday School; and Sister Ortiz by being the first person anyone goes to when they need a shoulder to cry on.

It is not simply those with the most obvious or the most visible gifts who bless the ward. It is each person doing her part in turn, even if her gifts are of the less-obvious variety. You might respond, *Yes, but Paul's teachings are the common heritage of all*

Christians—can't this same scenario play just as well in any Christian church, or in any church at all? To that I respond, *Perhaps.* It seems to me, however, that covenant Christian communities exert a special gravitational pull bringing us toward this ideal.

In my mind, there are at least two ways in which the restored Church of Jesus Christ distinctly pulls us toward one another. The first, as I've alluded to many times in this book, is the wonder of the many ways in which the Church kindly forces us into meaningful community with those who live close to us but from whom we may be very different.

I referenced Eugene England's enduring essay "Why the Church Is As True As the Gospel" in a previous chapter, but the essay bears quoting here. In the piece, England explains the genius of the many ways in which geographically defined wards change the complexion of our weekly religious experience. At one point in the essay, England talks about receiving a call to serve in a bishopric at BYU. He writes, apparently only half-jokingly, that "Ray [the bishop] is very different from me, a BYU business school conservative who I believed thought of me at that time as an impractical, liberal egghead—and I was sure he was a chauvinistic antiintellectual. It must have taken an angel with a drawn sword to convince him to call me." But then England goes on to detail the many ways in which they worked together and concludes that not only did they learn to love those they served together, but England himself came to love the bishop, too.[17]

England's essay is right in explaining that there is something radical about how both our lay clergy and the geographic organization of our wards prompt us to use our spiritual gifts in ways that are uniquely meaningful and beautiful. It has taken many years of living where Church members are few and far between for me to recognize how truly extraordinary our members are in their willingness to deliver such wholehearted devotion to their callings. Few parts of our worship impress me as more beautiful than the overworked accountant who nonetheless takes on the invisible and often thankless—but very time-consuming—role of ward financial secretary. Being financial secretary is not even a "pastoral" job in most senses, but one that allows members to bless the growth of the Church and the welfare of the poor by enabling the payment of tithing and offerings. By the same measure, I look at our current stake Relief Society president, a full-time physician and busy aunt and friend. On top of her already very busy life—visiting, blessing, helping, and healing—she organized our stake's response to the novel coronavirus pandemic, and that response has been magnificent.

Now, to be clear: all these people are imperfect. And those imperfections cannot be overlooked. My experience tells me that most Church members serving in lay callings do their level best, but even so, the process of shaping our spiritual lives together with others who are trying hard but constantly falling short can be genuinely frustrating and sometimes deeply difficult, especially because those other members all bring with them cultural, familial, and personal baggage that will sometimes limit their ability to serve. This process, then, is both messy and beautiful. Fully aware of each other's shortcomings, we come together, day, week, and year in and out, trying to cobble together a community in Christ. As we do so, we seek grace in forgiving our fellow Saints, just as we seek their forgiveness in our own moments of weakness. In so doing, we together provide an enduring testament to the Church's ability to leverage varying gifts to bless the body of Christ. Indeed, in one important sense, this devotion is a deep part of what makes the church "true and living."

There is a second way the restored Church renders us effective in sharing the gifts of Christ with those we love. My experience is that our Church, by precept and by covenant, in theology and in weekly practice, binds us by cords of empathy to those we love and serve. We've discussed previously Alma's formulation of our baptismal covenants as our being willing to commit "to mourn with those that mourn; yea, and comfort those that stand in need of comfort" (Mosiah 18:9). It is often precisely because we go to church every week and sit cheek to cheek and jowl to jowl with our fellow parishioners, because we serve them and are served by them, because we hold callings and are blessed by others in callings—in short, because we live a gospel life—that we care deeply about those who hurt. We cry with them when they cry, and we shout with them when they rejoice. A covenant life in the Church of Jesus Christ makes us acutely aware that sorrow anywhere in our congregations is our own, and it renders us better people because it helps us to care about others so organically. Such caring is possible in any organization, of course, and certainly in any church, but the fidelity with which we regularly attend is unusual.

Empathy is the beating heart at the center of a gospel life and constitutes one of the most beautiful blessings of the restored Church.

As stated before, we are obviously imperfect, but we are generally genuinely committed and willing to accept the call to serve. By covenant, commitment, and dedication, we demonstrate our willingness and ability to live up to the promises we make at baptism, to "succor the weak, lift up the hands which hang down, and strengthen the feeble knees" (D&C 81:5).

What's more, just as Paul, Moroni, and the Lord via Joseph Smith teach that it is in our incomplete state that we band together to find grace, perhaps there is something to be said for believing in a Church that is, in one sense, incomplete as well. Perhaps there is a divine purpose in leaving us with those "many great and important things" yet to come. Perhaps it is only in the context of a living and growing Church that we can band together to continue the pursuit of building Zion. In doing our duty—ministering, teaching, serving, lifting, and building—we become a true and living Church, indeed.

8

HEALING THE BODY
OF CHRIST

Questions

- I'm worried about the Church's approach to the marginalized, either because I feel marginalized myself or because I care about those who feel that way—where is my place?
- I wish the Church would speak out more forcefully on matters like racial equality and LGBTQ rights—what can I do?
- Can a church whose members and leaders in years past espoused racist views still be true? How can I approach that dissonance in a way that constructively disavows the problems while keeping my integrity intact?

In my discussions with young members of the Church who are seriously questioning whether to continue actively engaging in their Church membership, I have discovered that while some have intellectual questions resembling those we discussed in the book's first two sections, many others are reconsidering their Church membership because of matters of the heart. For some, these questions come because they do not feel comfortable at church. I could mention a host of examples—for instance, a gay man who sees little hope for a meaningful spiritual life within our religious tradition. Or an African American woman who notes that the members of her ward think that abandoning racism means merely not using racist epithets. Or a middle-aged woman, never married, who sees families surrounding her and wonders whether she really has a part to play in the kingdom of God.

Heartache in God's kingdom, however, increasingly does not extend just to those who feel excluded themselves. My experience and increasing amounts of data suggest that many, especially young members, who *do* fit the traditional mold of a fully engaged member of the Church feel heartsick *on behalf* of those who do not as easily fit in. I am thinking here of the *sister* of the gay man mentioned above, the *friend* of the African American woman, or the aging *parent* of the woman who has never married. Even beyond these close personal connections, we must think of those young people who worry that if *anyone anywhere* feels unwelcome in our Church, that fact alone suggests we are not what Christ needs us to be.

Increasingly, then, young Church members are reconsidering their relationship with the Church because they sense the Church does not offer a warm place of respite to all of God's children. Beyond concerns about historical narratives, an open canon, or imperfect prophets, these members feel integrity-bound to ensure they support only organizations that nourish the values that matter most to them. These members worry about the racialized treatments of members in years past and about the difficulty queer members still have in the Church today. In this calculus, the benefits of Church membership occupy a secondary role—which comes after determining whether Church activity and paying tithing potentially support an organization these people fear does not do enough to support and nourish all of its members, especially those who are marginalized.

I want to recognize up front that these are serious and deeply spiritual concerns. We cannot pass these worries over lightly. We cannot dismiss them. We cannot trivialize them. And they cannot go unaddressed. Indeed, as members of the Church, we must redouble our efforts to ensure that our covenant Christian communities offer respite, healing, and comfort to *all* those who stand in need.

In this chapter, I make no claims about being able to *solve* the deeply painful problems that attend these issues. I do, however, hope to offer some insights as to how we might think about these concerns, remain actively involved in Church service, and find our integrity intact.

MARGINALIZED MEMBERS

The word *marginalized* was virtually never used in common discourse before 1980, became somewhat popular in the 1990s, and more recently has become ubiquitous.[1] As I explained at the beginning of the book, I think this trend relates at least in part to the influence of the digital world. Rather than having mostly official or meta-narratives, now people have access to platforms where they see and hear all kinds of stories, places where we are all confronted with personal and previously less-represented voices. I'd also like to think that society in general is *striving* for more equity and fairness by trying to amplify these previously largely ignored lives and realities. Whatever the reasons, however, the world is now more aware of and generally sympathetic to marginalized communities than we were forty years ago.

And so it is, too, in the Church.

Again, I want to be clear: I do not know firsthand what it is like to be on the margins of the Church. To restate the point I made in the introduction: bearing witness to suffering is not the same as experiencing suffering. And while I listen intently and try to understand, I still know that I cannot really know what it is to be on the margins.

Even so: I am listening, and I am trying to understand. I believe many, many others in our Church community feel that way, too. Along with them, I wish desperately that the Church felt like a safe space for every person, regardless of the color of their skin, their sexual orientation, their experience of gender, their mental health, or their marital status. I wish that every ward were a refuge and a safe space where every person on earth could come to sup and find succor. I wish that we as the people of the Church better lived our theological commitments and that we would strive to be more like Zion.

To those striving disciples who feel, despite their best efforts, that they are looking in from the outside and are not ultimately welcome, please know that there are many people who care about you. Please know that you are a beloved child of God, even if you have sometimes been tragically made to feel otherwise. Please know that heavenly parents see, know, and love you.

And this all brings us to the heart of this book: if you feel marginalized within or by the Church, but you sense the Church is true or want to believe so in some capacity, can the Church still be a place to foster meaningful faith in Christ? Can you remain and keep your integrity intact?

That, I'm afraid, is a question only you can answer for yourself.

To be clear, I do *not* want this book, or anything I say, to be weaponized to force or manipulate those who feel marginalized to stay—even though I very much hope we can become a place where all such people feel welcome. The making of such a personal, weighty, and life-altering decision needs to be made in counsel with those you love and trust—those who, even if you decide to leave, will love, respect, and honor you, whatever your ultimate spiritual home.

For what it's worth, I look to those who do make it work as my great spiritual superiors. I think of an African American convert (whose story I will share in more detail below) who joined the church in the 1960s, and I marvel that he stuck with the Church for a decade before he could hold the priesthood or enter the temple. I think about gay Latter-day Saints who feel excluded but decide to stay anyway. I think of a woman with whom I've become good friends whose heart breaks because she feels unrepresented, but who nonetheless works to find a way to remain. And I think of the whip-smart Primary and Relief Society presidents who have very recently deeply blessed my life: both are single, and both, I must imagine, have passed through their own periods of difficulty in a church that often is, in many ways, built around families.

In each of these cases, I recognize that these people clear a high spiritual bar in a way I have never been asked to. My experience cannot encompass or even echo theirs. I can never pretend, with integrity, that I know how they feel. Instead, I can outline here some ideas for *all of us to think about.* These are the types of truths that could bring a measure of comfort to those who are suffering but which may simultaneously unsettle those who feel squarely comfortable in our pews.

EMPATHY AS A COVENANT VIRTUE

All of this brings us to one of the gospel's fundamental paradoxes: keeping our baptismal covenants in a bone-deep way may at times make staying actively engaged in Church service *harder*.

Surely one of scripture's most beautiful passages is the gathering of Alma's little band of Christian disciples at the edges of the waters of Mormon. We must remember the context—this is a small group of religious refugees hiding in the wilderness because their king despises their religious devotion. Given this, Alma's description of what their baptismal covenants will mean strikes at the very heart of the meaning of a disciple's life. In other words, he is preparing them to make the foundational covenant that will bind them together as believers fleeing persecution, and in doing so, he invites them not only to prepare themselves to stand as witnesses for God but also to tie themselves to one another in bonds of empathy, compassion, and service. In this context it can hardly surprise us that the roots of the English word *religion* quite literally mean to "again bind" ourselves—to God and to those around us (see Mosiah 18:8–10).

Thus it is that, within a ward, we celebrate births together—making meals for the suddenly sleep-deprived new parents. When a member of the congregation dies, we attend the funeral—yes, in remembrance of the deceased, but, more to the point, to throw our arms around those they have left behind, to soak up their tears on our shoulders. We watch together in these little communities as children grow and struggle and achieve and fail. As marriages prosper and fracture. As individuals flourish or flounder. And in our best incarnations we are not just there, but really *there* for all of it.

What is the call to "minister" if not an invitation to do just that?

Therefore we cannot say, "That queer woman's struggles are her own"; within our covenant Christian communities, there is no such thing as a sorrow that is meant to be born alone. If a Black man, or a queer woman, or a single man, or a transgender woman, or a new immigrant, or any other person comes to one of our religious communities with a heart full of sorrow, we are not merely invited to take this weight upon us; we have covenanted to do so, sealing that promise by our disappearance into the waters of baptism. As President Jean B. Bingham taught, "Our responsibility is to extend an open hand and heart. As we do that, we find that we have created a safe place for sharing, a safe place to grow, a safe place to become our best selves."[2]

I am reminded of a deeply spiritual hour I recently spent as part of the institute class I help to teach here on campus. Darius Gray—the African American man who joined the Church in the 1960s and who I briefly referenced above—spoke to us on a Friday in November 2020 and spent most of his time not opining or outlining abstract principles but instead telling us stories. Brother Gray converted to The Church of Jesus Christ of Latter-day Saints many years before the 1978 revelation extending priesthood and temple blessings to Black members, and he has become one of the leading voices on racial reconciliation in the Church. He recounted how as a young man he met the missionaries and, against his mother's advice, decided to take the discussions and learn about the gospel. He had a vague idea about the priesthood restriction as he learned, but he knew few details about it. Just days before he was to be baptized, however, he learned about it in much greater detail and was understandably shocked and offended.

Equipped with that knowledge, Darius changed his mind and decided not to join.

The next day, however, lying alone on his bed, looking up through the window at the stars, he heard a voice say distinctly in his mind, "This is Christ's restored Church, and you are to join."

Taken aback, he carefully considered, and the next day followed the Spirit's direction and was baptized.

The day after his baptism, Brother Gray was informed that he would be asked to share some remarks in sacrament meeting. Unsure how he would do such a thing, he approached some members for instructions: they told him how to open and how to close but said nothing about what he should say in the middle. Nervous at the prospect of speaking in front of so many people, Darius went to the cultural hall to pace, taking some time for himself to think. As he walked the open space, a young girl ran into the room with an exuberant smile on her face, running as if right toward him. Yet after looking up and seeing his face, she ran the other direction, out back through the door, and, as she did, Brother Gray heard her shout to her mother, "Look, Mom, it's a ******."

When Brother Gray told this story, we all sat there in pained silence. Here was a young man, fighting against every instinct and every prevailing cultural suggestion, summoning the courage to follow the voice of the Spirit in joining a church that at that time would not allow him access to its lay priesthood or its holiest rites. Here he was, bravely coming to the chapel and preparing to speak for the first time. We would hope he would have been welcomed into the ward—but instead, he heard the English language's most offensive racial epithet.

This episode happened more than fifty years ago, yet hearing it retold cut me to the quick and left me terribly upset, desperate to help.

In the same vein, I remember becoming good friends with a young undergraduate student while I was in the bishopric of our Young Single Adult ward—let's call her Jennifer. Jennifer and I would take walks around campus, during which we would discuss life and God. More than anything else, however, the questions that haunted this friend were queries like, "Why can't women be better represented in leading councils of the Church?" and, "Why can't we hear from more women in general conference?" To her, fully engaged as she was in a world where gender equity was the striving norm, the glaring lack of gender equity in many aspects of the Church and its management stung. Her thoughts reflect sentiments similar to those of Church convert and scholar CarrieAnne Simonini DeLoach. In remembering the sting of being nearly the only woman in her armed forces sacrament services, she wrote:

> In [these meetings] I was almost always the only attendee without the priesthood. In neither, I discovered, were probing questions on gender inequality welcome. My intentions in pursuing such inquiry were not to be provocative or to draw undue attention to my ignorance. I wanted access to the strength and connectivity patriarchal histories and priesthood pedigrees provided as the sinew between living men and male generations in the priesthood body of faith. I, too, wanted a theology as specific as my role and as expansive as the generations of women linking me to my Heavenly Mother.[3]

Brother Gray's and Jennifer's stories expose deep, ponderous, theological questions. Some young people, for instance, wonder how God's true Church could have a policy denying those with African ancestry access to temples and the priesthood. These young people ask me plaintively: "Can 'God's Church' really be God's if we are still constrained by the cords of racist folklore and a narrow worldview?" Similarly, is our Church doing all it can—are we, to paraphrase Elder Maxwell, using "whatever stretch there may be in [our theological] tethers"[4] to ensure women are heard and valued? What do we lose when women are not given positions of independent authority, or when women are considered accessories to making decisions?

And whatever the answers to those questions, we must recognize that great sorrow has flowed because of the times when we, as Church members, have failed to recognize and honor the full divinity within each of our brothers and sisters.

These questions matter deeply, and they require working through again and again and again in our hearts and minds. And, *while we work*—in whatever limited capacities we have as lay members—we can simultaneously strive to demonstrate our willingness to live the covenants we made when we entered the waters of baptism. Within the gospel framework, after all, only very few members are called to sit in judgment. But literally every member of the Church has covenanted to empathize with our fellow parishioners.

Thus, concern for the vulnerable who suffer within our congregations is not a peripheral issue. Focusing on empathy for the marginalized—and especially those who feel that way within the Church—is not a *dilution* but a *distillation* of our doctrine.

Indeed, as in all things in the gospel, Christ is our perfect exemplar. Indeed, what constitutes the beating heart of the Atonement of Jesus Christ more than the perfect love that led Christ to enter with willing empathy into the suffering of all God's children? I am not saying that empathy constitutes the entirety of the Atonement—the scriptures make it clear that the Atonement's functions are myriad and complex. Nevertheless, I remain convinced that whether we look to Christ bleeding under the weight of the world in the Garden of Gethsemane or to God weeping before Enoch over humanity, one of the virtues that most defines the character of divinity is a consistent, organic, natural inclination toward empathy.[5]

And He invites us to do and be likewise—most especially

toward those in our immediate congregations who are suffering and feel pushed toward the margins.

BINDING UP THE BODY OF CHRIST

Yet, for all the foregoing talk about empathy as a covenant virtue, I sense many young people will remain troubled. The heartache that underlies this consternation derives chiefly from two sources. First, it is quite simply a weighty burden to feel responsible for sharing these heavy loads, especially if other members of the congregation seem blind to them. Second, this emotional weight also brings with it intellectual concern. Wouldn't we hope that the Church of Jesus Christ would have within it *no one* who feels marginalized? Or at least that it would not facilitate or exacerbate such marginalization?

These are serious and meaningful questions. And I will address both, starting with the second one.

During the summer of upheaval following the death of George Floyd in 2020, like many of us, I felt a great deal of angst concerning these questions. I wanted desperately to know how I might contribute to the solution that would end systemic racism, and I certainly did not want to contribute even unintentionally to the problem. What's more, as a young bishop, I felt responsible to think deeply through these issues on behalf of the members of my flock I knew were also deeply troubled. One night, feeling the weight of these injustices keenly, if only vicariously, I wrote an email to Dr. David Holland, whose thoughts on spiritual matters I value greatly. As part of that email, I wrote the following:

> I feel morally compelled to better address racism, and want our Church to move toward a Zion where "black and white, bond and free, male and female" are genuinely treated equally. I want our Church to wade into this moral

fray and to call for systemic change. George Floyd reminds us that the world is not there yet, and the experiences of many members of color from within our own congregations (and at BYU) tell us the Church is not there yet, either. Your dad's clarion call in last conference notwithstanding, it would be like water in the desert for many of our young to hear talk after talk in conference about the need to fight racism and prejudice of every kind.[6]

Dr. Holland's answer back was swift and read, in part,

> For me, one of the great metaphors for the Church is the story of the brother of Jared. I imagine when he discovered the stones, they still reflected the setting in which they were found. Remarkably clear and brilliant in many ways, but still containing the imperfections and impurities of the circumstances in which they came to be, they could not shine until touched by Grace. I have no doubt that this Church picked up the imperfections of its setting and cannot fully provide light until some of these things are purified by His touch. In doing so, I don't think that will undermine people's faith in its divine mission; rather they will see a church that demonstrates that faith, repentance, and endurance in the light that it is trying to help its members live.

I love Dr. Holland's metaphor. Part of what reaches me deeply about the story of the brother of Jared trying to light his barges is the contrast between how hard the brother of Jared is apparently trying and the manifest and categorical insufficiency of his offering.

The Lord in effect asks the brother of Jared to do his best in procuring something to light the ships that will soon be submerged under the roiling ocean waves.

And what does the brother of Jared bring in return?

Some rocks.

Again, I am not questioning the brother of Jared's sincerity. I imagine I would have done no better. Moreover, accounting for the ambiguity of how the stones were made and what exactly they looked like, it stands to reason he may have poured his whole soul into making them.

And yet, in the final analysis: rocks are rocks.

And rocks are not going to provide light to anybody.

That all further reinforces Dr. Holland's point. At the end of the day, any offering that any of us individually brings to the Lord will always be hopelessly and categorically insufficient. The divinity that illuminates any of our individual offerings springs not from the offerings themselves but from the grace infused into them by the Lord. Thus, when Nephi teaches it is "by grace that we are saved, after all we can do" (2 Nephi 25:23), he elides the fact that the "all" may be indeed very small.

Given how that prophetic example stands as an archetype for all the offerings we individually bring to God, it should not surprise us that the Church we bring Him collectively also needs to be suffused with His grace to become what He means it to be. We are all subject to the cultural forces that shape and bind us—the Church collectively, as well as each of us individually. To rise above these collective cultural constraints, we must muster the shared humility to seek the grace that will move us toward Zion.

Indeed, in precisely this vein we read these plaintive words from the brother of Jared as he brings the stones to the Lord, asking for His touch:

> O Lord, thou hast said that we must be encompassed about by the floods. Now behold, O Lord, and do not be angry with thy servant because of his weakness before thee; for we know that thou art holy and dwellest in the heavens, and that we are unworthy before thee; because of the

fall our natures have become evil continually; nevertheless, O Lord, thou hast given us a commandment that we must call upon thee, that from thee we may receive according to our desires.

. . . O Lord, look upon me in pity, and turn away thine anger from this thy people, and suffer not that they shall go forth across this raging deep in darkness; but behold these things which I have molten out of the rock.

And I know, O Lord, that thou hast all power, and can do whatsoever thou wilt for the benefit of man; therefore touch these stones, O Lord, with thy finger, and prepare them that they may shine forth in darkness; and they shall shine forth unto us in the vessels which we have prepared, that we may have light while we shall cross the sea. (Ether 3:2–4)

The brother of Jared seems close to embarrassment in these verses—clearly, deeply, even achingly uncomfortable with the paltry offering he has brought to be blessed by the touch of the Master's hand. And in that discomfort, I hear our collective sorrow as we offer to the Lord a church that so often falls so short of the Zion we have been called to build. Together, we kneel before the Lord, and in effect pray to Him,

> *O Lord, we recognize that the body of the Church is still tainted with racism and riven by class; we know that members and leaders alike are constrained by the bonds of culture, and that our vision is limited by our ability to see beyond our own provincial borders. And yet we bring to Thee this offering with full purpose of heart and a genuine depth of sincerity and ask Thee, despite our individual and collective shortcomings, to touch this Church and make it shine.*

That is not a prayer we make once just before getting it all right. No; this is our constant, collective call—the desire of imperfect but striving Christian disciples who are trying so hard to get it right even while knowingly and unknowingly falling far short of the mark.

These ideas bring us back to the first question: but what of the burden that is born by members who feel marginalized themselves and by those who reach out to the marginalized in empathy?

I have been privileged during my many years in the Church to know some of the people who resplendently exemplify carrying this burden with grace. One such example came to me briefly but with great force and power. I mentioned above the hour our institute class spent with Darius Gray. During that hour, I was at first horrified and brokenhearted to hear of the terrible way Brother Gray had sometimes been treated after joining the Church. Very soon, however, I found my own broken heart bound back together by the manifest grace Brother Gray demonstrated in describing how he had moved past these various affronts. Brother Gray was not haunted by lingering resentment, nor was he burdened by waiting for apologies.

Rather, with eminent kindness and an endowment of grace, he had transcended the pain and—in a way I find difficult to describe—emanated light as a result. Brother Gray has every right to be bitter. He could easily have left the Church; or, if he decided to stay, he could have lorded his pain over the members who originally caused it or over those who maintain racist attitudes or cause racialized pain. But he has instead chosen a path of healing that transcends such concerns. I am not suggesting Brother Gray overlooks the hard stuff—far from it. He speaks with candor and bluntness. He tells stories in their naked difficulty—such as the one I quoted above. But precisely because of that candor, his grace and his forgiveness shine all the brighter. His entire life is a testament to the healing power of divine grace in moving beyond real hurt and sorrow, even when that sorrow comes from within the Church.

Another example of bearing these burdens comes from a woman—I'll call her Elissa—whom I have come to know very well over the years. She has earned a reputation in this neck of the woods as "the patron saint of gay Bay Area Church members." Over many years now, she has become known as a safe place, a refuge to whom gay Church members can turn. In so doing, her heart has been filled to overflowing and has broken on more than one occasion. Without any special calling or designation, she has ministered to those in need again and again and again. She has sat with gay Church members as they've opened their hearts and offered her their pain. She has never offered judgment but has been a consistent and affirming source of love. Her love is not political or showy, but instead quiet and nurturing, open and honest, welcoming and divine. She is often opening herself to their pain and sorrow and heartache, more than once weeping with them through the night and, per their own accounts, saving more than one life in the process.

My point here is not to paint any of those I have described as perfect or having figured it all out—none of them would claim that. But I do mean to suggest that these members, whether marginalized themselves or whether reaching out to those on the margins, possess a special spiritual gift—one without which the Church simply could not function. Their gift is the ability to bind wounds. These are they who nurse back to health the body of Christ when it is injured. These are they who are not afraid to face an open wound in all its gritty gore and foul stench. These are they who pour oil and aloe into the hurting places and who quietly, carefully, and deliberately succor Christ's wounded body until it mends.

The irony is that these same members sometimes face scrutiny or even ostracization at the hands of others who think they are overly tolerant. Sadly, some of these special healers must labor on not only without recognition but sometimes in the face of opposition from within the body of the Church. Yet I am convinced that just as much as the Church needs great teachers, and Relief Society presidents, and bishops, and Apostles, it also desperately needs these healers. Of course, sometimes these are one and the same.

And so, here I issue an admittedly difficult challenge. If you find yourself reconsidering your relationship to the Church because your heart has broken over and over again at the suffering of the marginalized within the body of Christ, perhaps it is worth considering whether that is precisely the reason to stay.

WHEN THE CHURCH CRIES OUT IN PAIN

My oldest son, ten years old, seems to have been born a thirty-year-old existentialist philosopher. He will often go into a reverie of sorts in which he looks out the window of the car and sits silently for long moments. Then, suddenly, he will emerge from the quiet and say something startling, sometimes even profound.

In the spring of 2022, he was having one of those moments when he suddenly came back to the reality around him, looked at me, and said, "Dad, two of the most important things in the world are pain and death." I've been his dad long enough to know when he says something like that it is better to probe his thinking before responding with panic and dread (which is usually my first inclination). When I asked him to explain, he said, "Well, Dad, there are already seven billion people on the planet, and if some of them don't die there will be like seventy billion, and the world can barely take care of us as it is—so some people need to die. And, if you cut your foot but there was no pain, you would get an infection, and you could get really sick. So, see, pain and death matter a lot."

I was brought up short.

My son's future as a philosopher aside, he was undoubtedly right on this point: pain is important to keeping us healthy. It serves as a warning, a red flag. It is the body's way of saying, "Here is a problem that needs to be addressed." Because it is so important, it's hardly surprising to note that the body has developed a beautiful and complex system for making sure that pain signals travel quickly from the body's periphery to the brain (which can then respond in kind).

If you puncture your toe on a nail (ouch), there are special receptors in the toe that immediately fire a specific kind of electrical impulse to the nearest nerve fibers. That impulse is then propagated along that first fiber and then through a series of nerves, crossing multiple inter-nerve junctions along the way, until it arrives, in well under a second, at the brain. Once there, the brain has learned to interpret that particular kind of impulse from that specific kind of neuron as horribly unpleasant, and, absent a reason to do otherwise, your body will recoil from the cause of the pain.

Why am I giving you this short lecture on neurology? Because this explanation underlies the most helpful analogy I've ever heard regarding one of the hardest questions we must ask as disciples: what should we do when the body of Christ, the Church, is hurting?

There are multiple answers, but the one I want to focus on first is based on an analogy given by Dr. David Holland (I recognize I'm quoting him again; he has had a profound impact on my thinking in these matters) in a personal interview many years ago. He told me that while most of us are not called to function as part of the "brain" of the Church (that is, general Church leaders), and while I may be only a metaphorical finger in the body of Christ, even as a finger I have a *responsibility* to convey pain signals to the "brain."

Let me elaborate on what I believe this analogy does—and

does not—mean for a regular member like me. Membership in the Church is almost certain to involve some amount of friction. There will be times when we disagree with what our leaders do—whether that's the theme the bishop chooses for ward conference, the way the stake conducts the Pioneer Trek, or something central coming down from Church headquarters in Salt Lake City.

In many cases, the resulting friction may be of little moral moment and may be relatively little cause for concern. All of us must learn to overlook some such minor annoyances as part of the price of living in a thriving community. But other concerns are not so easily dismissed. There may be times when, like a finger held against a hot burner, we sense real, deep, and damaging pain—and when this happens, our conscience cries out that we must do something, both for our own integrity and for the good of the body of Christ.

In this context, I believe we can find some meaningful recourse in the organization of the local church. When we are confronted with these deeply difficult issues, the Lord has provided a way for us to address them constructively and meaningfully—by talking with our local leaders. Speaking on just this subject—and warning against what he called "activism toward the church"—Brother Ahmad Corbitt, of the Young Men General Presidency, counseled that when members have deep concerns about policies of the Church, they should speak with their local leaders: "humbly and lovingly expressing concerns, sharing observations, even lodging formal complaints."[7]

Now, I want to acknowledge that this may seem like thin gruel to many members. In part, this is because local leaders, too, are imperfect. Some leaders will not respond with empathy and some local leaders may even interpret these discussions as demonstrating a lack of faith. I acknowledge, as Elder Uchtdorf and Elder Holland have (as quoted in previous chapters), that the imperfection of local leaders can make these matters even more difficult. What's more, even when local leaders do respond with empathy, we may feel that this does little good since, after all, what power does a bishop or stake president have to make a difference in the wider Church?

But in response to this second objection, I would offer two observations. The first is that 95 percent of a member's *actual lived experience in the Church* happens not in the Church Office Building or the Conference Center in Salt Lake but in a local meetinghouse. Which is to say, while a bishop does not declare Church doctrine, he can faithfully *implement* Church policy with an eye toward the needs of his congregation—indeed, that is a local leader's job. This is not to suggest local leaders make up their own doctrine or draw up their own way of doing things but simply to recognize that the local implementation of Church policy necessarily depends on local needs. The other response that matters here is this: just as individual neurons can combine into a chorus of neural signals that eventually carry an overwhelming signal to the brain, comments shared in good faith with local leaders, if echoed across the Church, can likewise combine into a signal that the Church's "central nervous system" needs to hear.

But that also brings us to a difficult—and necessary—truth. One the one hand, if I am but a finger in the body of Christ, I have a responsibility to be the best darn finger I can be and to transmit pain signals when integrity demands that I do so. At the same time, as a finger, I must also understand that I am not the brain. And that understanding may at times necessitate accepting that the brain will make decisions that seem counterintuitive, challenging, or that even seem harmful. In some cases, this may be because the brain is still carefully seeking further understanding before responding to the pain. In some cases, this is because the brain sees a more complete picture than I do, and what seems harmful to me is not, when understood in broader context. And in some cases, I will find that the pain I sense is real, and the brain will respond in kind.

But one aspect of faith involves accepting that transmitting my pain up the nerve fibers does not guarantee the outcome I desire—and acknowledging that that may be because what I desire is either not possible or would not in fact help, even though I may believe it would. In this sense, I have come to think of meeting with my local leader like this: expressing the pain I feel and doing so with candor and faith can be an act of consecration. That pain is something I lay on the altar, consecrating it to God and praying that it will be considered carefully (even if by people who are imperfect) and that the "brain" of the Church will act in a way that aligns with the will of God and honors my experience and my truth.

In my mind, one of the most important examples of this process working in the Church came in relation to the 2015 policy that excluded the children of gay couples from baptism and baby blessings (except with special permission). It is well known that this policy caused a great deal of heartache; I know that in my area it was an earthquake the likes of which we had not seen in many years in the Church. What most strikes me, however, is that after the policy was reversed, President Nelson spoke with great candor about the process that led to the reversal—and what he outlines very much mirrors what we discussed above. Speaking to BYU students after the policy had been reversed in 2019, he said the following:

> The First Presidency and Quorum of the Twelve have continued to seek the Lord's guidance and to plead with Him on behalf of His children who were affected by the 2015 policy. *We knew that this policy created concern and confusion for some and heartache for others. That grieved us.*

Whenever the sons and daughters of God weep—for whatever reasons—we weep.[8]

Importantly, his words demonstrate that sincerely conveying pain signals "up the nerves" to the central nervous system is *not* "murmuring." The kind of respectful, candid, and transparent acknowledgment of pain that I'm talking about here is not that and is, in fact, integral to the health of the body of Christ.

Similarly, while we often talk of revelation in the Church as if it must arise in a vacuum, precisely the opposite is almost always the case. In a letter to his son describing the principles underlying the origin of revelation in the Church, President Spencer W. Kimball wrote, "Revelations will probably never come unless they are desired. I think few people receive revelations while lounging on the couch or while playing cards or while relaxing. I believe most revelations would come when a man is on his tip toes, reaching as high as he can for something which he knows he needs, and then there bursts upon him the answer to his problems."[9] As has been recounted in the exhaustively researched article and book chapter written by Edward Kimball about the process of his father's 1978 revelation, much of the origin for the revelation flowed precisely from the fact that President Kimball had been touched over decades by the righteous longing of Black Church members to have the blessings of the temple and the priesthood.

Now, I must recognize three things. First, we must be candid and clear that sending our pleadings and cries of pain to the brain does *not* guarantee the outcome we desire, let alone on a swift timeline. To begin with, the Church is a complex organization, and multiple pleas may come from multiple places, and there may be good reasons for each. Further, as President Nelson and others have explained, Church leaders are not at liberty to change doctrine or policy just because members—or even they themselves—think those changes would be a good idea. The article detailing the origin of the 1978 revelation makes clear that the process of arriving at the revelation was long and torturous. President Kimball wanted to know that he moved because of revelation, not public pressure.

The second thing is a small aside to local Church leaders. Before saying this I want to recognize that I have no place or authority to give ecclesiastical counsel. Having said that, I think what I will say here can be fairly inferred from both the ecclesiastical structure of the Church and recent prophetic direction. The idea is this: local leaders must lovingly pass "pain signals" up the nervous system so they can arrive at the brain. It is our job to make sure the central nervous system knows what is happening to the far-flung limbs of the Church. Indeed, in the above example, part of the reason that President Nelson, by his own description, could respond in the way he and other Church leaders did was precisely because the pain signals were passed along to them. It strikes me as helpful and potentially healing for local Church leaders to make sure members know such signals are welcome—and that those members are safe in sharing them.

Third, as Church members, we must recognize that sending pain signals up the nerve fibers does not constitute our only job. In addition—and certainly just as importantly—we are to labor to heal the body of Christ *right where we are*. We do this work individually by loving and loving and loving and loving some more. For most Church members, we have no obligation or responsibility to judge others. We do, however, have covenantal responsibilities to love those around us, to center the marginalized, and to "lift up the hands which hang down" (D&C 81:5).

And, even more so, we are likewise called to use whatever stewardship we have in the Church to ensure we accomplish those same purposes. I'm brought in this regard to think of a dear bishop our family had who, upon his installation into that calling, gave a beautiful talk titled "A Seat at the Table." The chorus he echoed again and again and again was this: "No matter who you are, no matter how you identify, no matter who you love or what you look like—you are welcome here. We offer you a seat of honor at the head of the table in this ward. We need you. Please come."

Yet one does not need to be a bishop to make that kind of effort. One can do it as a teacher, a Young Women president, a ministering brother or sister, a Primary worker, or virtually anywhere else. Whatever we do in the Church, we are called to use our stewardships and our councils to build Zion. Indeed, when we feel most acutely the gap between who we are and who God needs us to be, we would do well to remember that the best way for us to shrink that gap is to do all we can locally to make the Church more like Zion. Insofar as the gospel word for change is repentance, this is an area where all of us have room to repent.

WE MUST BE THE CHANGE
WE WISH TO SEE IN THE WORLD

I'm brought to think of the need for this kind of collective repentance when I think of the racism that still infects too much of the Church. I bring up racism in this context precisely because this is an area where so much good and important work remains to be done. All of us can do better to make the Church a warm and welcoming place for all people, their country of origin and skin color notwithstanding. The example of race can stand as a symbol for the good we can do—with local efforts mattering most—to move the Church toward Zion.

The full blessings of the gospel have been open to all Church members for forty-five years now, and Church leaders have made it clear in recent years that battling racism is an ongoing and urgent priority. Indeed, in a tweet sent in the aftermath of George Floyd's death, President Nelson called us, precisely, to "repent" and "abandon attitudes of prejudice."[10] Still, I worry that too many of us blithely pass by this prophetic invitation, supposing that it applies to others, but not to us.

Helping to dispel the myth that racism is not still a problem in the Church are the experiences of students of color at BYU. In the summer of 2020, students of color described their experiences at BYU with candor and transparency. Perhaps no other student's words left me as disappointed in the failure of all of us to address these issues in the Church as the words of Déborah Aléxis, the outgoing president of BYU's Black Student Union. She wrote, "Black students expect that attending a Church-run school that ostensibly adheres to Christ's teachings will be an uplifting and affirming experience. We are stunned and devastated when we discover the contrary." She went on to observe:

> Students privileged to not be affected by the racial isolation on our campus or in our church are often exasperated with our demands for change. Their lack of historical awareness of racism in our church and consequently on our campus renders them ignorant and apathetic to dismantling the continuation of white supremacy.[11]

At the time she wrote those words in June 2020, some in the Church might have quibbled that she was being "overdramatic" or that perhaps her experience might not reflect that of most students of color at BYU.

But any question about the widespread nature of such experiences was put to rest in February 2021, when BYU itself released the findings and recommendations of its own presidentially commissioned committee on race and inclusion at BYU. The report demonstrated that not only was BYU becoming progressively less diverse over time, but that the few minority students who attended had drastically worse outcomes than their peers and, unsurprisingly, felt besieged, isolated, and often downright attacked as a result. Both Alexis specifically and the summary of the report in general singled out BYU religion classes as an area of particular concern. The authors of the BYU report wrote:

> Many BIPOC (Black, Indigenous, and People of Color) students reported that some of the most hurtful experiences they have had occurred in religion courses, where sensitive gospel topics such as the priesthood and temple ban and skin color in the Book of Mormon can be misunderstood or insensitively presented. In classes across campus, students have felt they cannot always count on their instructors to effectively navigate these difficult issues in the classroom, and they have noted that some White students feel emboldened to make hurtful remarks on the issue of race.[12]

Now, of course, most Church members are not BYU students, and many never were or will be. So, in that sense, one could argue that we ought not focus too much on the experience of BYU students generally or in religion classes specifically. Furthermore, I am friends with multiple BYU professors, some of whom teach religion there—and I know them to be deeply good, thoroughly committed Saints who want desperately to do what's right and to help students in every way they know how.

But I bring these examples up here for a specific reason: no other place on earth represents in such concentrated form the experiences of Church membership as BYU. Brigham Young University effectively acts as an ambassador from the Church to the wider (especially academic) world. And it would stand to reason that BYU religion classes, of all places, should represent the pinnacle of religious education in the Church. This is just to say that if the experience of members of color is as reflected here, then we know that we as a church have a deep need to better understand and appreciate the extent of racism within our midst. This is an urgent problem with real consequences.

Professor Ryan Gabriel, in a devotional at BYU, taught these attendant truths powerfully:

> Yet the adversary attempts to distort the great commandment through pernicious forms of racism. He attempts to convince us that if we want a world in which race is no longer a contributing factor to how various groups are treated, then we need to stop focusing on race. This perspective might work if we lived in an ideal society without a history of slavery, convict leasing, and lynching. Nevertheless, we live in a fallen world, a world that has historical sins that reverberate into today. . . . [Christ] does not ask us to deny another's pain but to know it and touch it. To deny the genuine pain of another is to deny the very suffering Christ felt for them privately in the Garden of Gethsemane and publicly upon the cross at Calvary.[13]

We seem to reflect the flaws of a different group of our predecessors—the people of Zarahemla to whom Alma went to preach in Alma 5. This sermon is readily understood as a personal inventory—an interview to have with ourselves. But in the context the Book of Mormon offers us, I believe it also serves as a call for us to remember that the way we treat the marginalized deeply matters. Indeed, there are moments where the sermon calls us to collectively strive for a more just world. Alma calls the people to whom he is preaching to recognize the many ways in which they have begun to divide themselves along racial, financial, and other lines—and to mend these divisions.

Moreover, in Alma 4, Mormon indicates that it was precisely

the divisions among the people that convinced Alma to give up his political post to pursue a full-time prophetic ministry. We read that the people of the Church "began to be lifted up in the pride of their eyes, and to set their hearts upon riches and upon the vain things of the world" (Alma 4:8); as a consequence, we read that "there were envyings, and strife, and malice, and persecutions, and pride, even to exceed the pride of those who did not belong to the church of God" (v. 9); and finally, we come to the crushing blow, the one that I might imagine was the final blow in convincing Alma to give up his day job: "And the wickedness of the church was a great stumbling-block to those who did not belong to the church; and thus the church began to fail in its progress . . . *the example of the church* began to lead those who were unbelievers on from one piece of iniquity to another, thus bringing on the destruction of the people" (vv. 10–11; emphasis added).

And what did the people outside the Church do once they felt freed to mimic the actions of those within it? Alma "saw great inequality among the people, some lifting themselves up with their pride, despising others, turning their backs upon the needy and the naked and those who were hungry, and those who were athirst, and those who were sick and afflicted" (Alma 4:12).

Because I'd passed over these verses so easily so many times before, I'm going to invite us to go back and reread the last paragraph. Note who is being condemned here. Note whose behavior leads Alma to leave to preach to the city of Zarahemla. And then note that chapter 5 begins with Mormon recounting that "these are the words which he spake *to the people in the church*" (Alma 5:2; emphasis added). Given this context, we can hardly be surprised that among the many questions Alma asks his audience are these: "Are ye stripped of pride?" "[Have ye] been sufficiently humble?" "Is there one among you who is not stripped of envy?" "Is there one among you that doth make a mock of his brother, or that heapeth upon him persecutions?" (Alma 5:28, 27, 29, 30).

Let that sink in for a moment.

We must consider our own answers to these penetrating questions.

Do we, with misguided zeal meant to defend the power of the principles of the restored gospel, alienate the very people to whom the gospel is supposed to go? Do we, thinking about defending Brigham Young (or whomever) but ignoring Christ's plea and commandment to "love thy neighbour as thyself" (Matthew 22:39), fail to recognize where we still hold racial animus? Do we believe that protecting racist folklore matters more than abandoning pride or more than making the Church a safe space for all? As scholar and author Robert Rees has written, "Shedding racism is not like taking off a coat. It lies deep in the cells of the body, the dendrites of the brain, the chambers of the heart and the dark recesses of the soul."[14]

In pondering our own history with racism as individuals and as a church, we finally arrive at the full majesty and power of an open canon and a living Church:

They allow us to know we were wrong.

And this recognition need not fell our testimonies because prophetic or ecclesiastical or religious perfection is not necessary in a community founded on the perfect love and saving grace of the Redeemer, Jesus Christ. We need not ignore the sins of our predecessors—whether they be prophets or ordinary people just like us. Through the Atonement of Jesus Christ, all of us—Nephi, Mormon, Moroni, Brigham Young, and even you and me—can be made perfect. Raised in a world beholden to mortal systems of caste and race, ethnicity and class, we can rise above and recognize even places where our Church has become infected with—and must now escape from—these same deadly cultural viral strains.

The promise of the open canon is the declaration that the sweep of Christ's Atonement extends in all its majesty and power to include not just individuals, but generations, churches, and even the Lord's covenant people, be they ancient Israel, the Church in Zarahemla, or The Church of Jesus Christ of Latter-day Saints.[15]

Indeed, in this notion we return from the open canon to the true and living Church. Recall the importance of that latter word: *living*. Often, when we speak of what makes our Church worth joining, we talk about the truth. We discuss a foundation of prophets and apostles, and we emphasize again and again and again the veracity of our doctrine and the nobility of our history.

But in addition to those foundational truths, *we are the Church*. God will invite but not compel. He will command but not force. He will show us the way but cannot make us follow. And so, over and over again—throughout ancient scripture, and again starting in Missouri in the 1830s—the Lord has called His people to build Zion.

And almost as often, we have failed to live up to His vision because we cannot bring ourselves to abandon our love for the many ways in which we hope to claim superiority. Like the people of Zarahemla, we love dividing ourselves based on race, or class, or education, or income, or house size, or any of an almost infinite number of other factors, more than we long to establish Zion.

Yet for the Lord's people, Zion will always beckon.

It calls to us from the horizon, no matter how distant the view.

9

BELIEVING AND BECOMING

Questions

- What is the point of believing?
- Do Church members continue in faith just because they want to keep believing what they've always believed?
- How can Church membership change who I am?

Our discussion throughout this book has likely made it clear—in case there were any doubt when you picked it up—that the journey of Christian faith is not for the faint of heart. Walking the path toward the tree of life is just as Lehi and Nephi told us it would be—it requires discipline and determination and will likely exhaust us, requiring the last full measure of our devotion.

All of this discussion, then, leads us to a final set of questions that animate the entire motivation for taking the journey in the first place—just what it is we are seeking? Is the point of life to be able to honestly affirm historical truth-claims? Is life a complicated philosophical or abstract theological exercise? Is this all a matter of what happens between our ears? The scriptures speak clearly to these questions. It is to these answers that we will now turn.

FAITH IS ABOUT BECOMING

For all the emphasis the scriptures give to developing faith, they also teach us this core truth: alone, it lies inert. Hope, meekness, and charity give faith life. Thus, as Moroni contemplates ending the Nephite record, he quotes the words of his father, Mormon:

> Wherefore, if a man have faith he must needs have hope; for without faith there cannot be any hope. And again, behold I say unto you that he cannot have faith and hope, save he shall be meek, and lowly of heart. . . . and if a man be meek and lowly in heart, and confesses by the power of the Holy Ghost that Jesus is the Christ, he must needs have charity; for if he have not charity he is nothing; wherefore he must needs have charity. . . . Wherefore, my beloved brethren, pray unto the Father with all the energy of heart, that ye may be filled with this love. (Moroni 7:42–44, 48)

In other words: faith is not an academic or purely cognitive exercise. Ultimately, though epistemological confidence matters, such confidence is a necessary means but not an end. We are not here on earth attempting to procure sufficient confidence in a list of certain truth-claims. Rather, the truth-claims matter because prophets and scriptures are meant to draw our eyes to God, and as we come to know God, that closeness changes who we are.

Faith keeps our diligence aloft when we doubt—meaning it's not an irrational acceptance of fanciful claims but the fuel that powers our discipleship during times when our confidence flags. By buoying our diligence during those difficult times, faith becomes the force that allows us access to the power of the Atonement such that our character and impulses change—it is the wellspring of becoming like Christ.

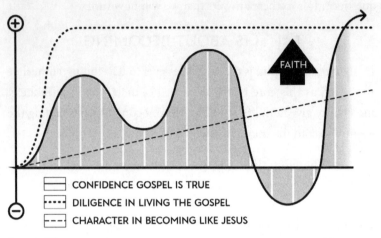

Graph #7

With this graph in mind, we can return to an idea we covered in some detail earlier in the book but whose importance now becomes fully apparent. The chief reason that continued spiritual diligence matters in the face of undulating uncertainty is because only that level of discipline allows us enough longitudinal access to the power of grace to allow our characters to develop as they must if we are to become like Jesus.

This truth matters deeply.

JUST WHAT IS RELIGION, ANYWAY?

Before continuing with the thread of this argument directly, I want to share two stories to help illustrate a point. The first story is my own and involves a frying pan. The second is Albert Einstein's and involves the nature of light.

Story #1: Early in our family life, as best I can remember, we owned a single frying pan. That wasn't much of a problem because our kitchen was a few burners, a sink, and about four square feet of countertop. That pan was covered in Teflon, and I loved it because it was so easy to make scrambled eggs.

Sometime shortly after we moved to California, we found ourselves with a (still small but) significantly better kitchen, and we decided it was time to upgrade and expand our cooking repertoire. I went out to Target and bought a gleaming, new, stainless steel frying pan. It *looked* as though it would scramble the most beautiful eggs I'd ever eaten. I still remember getting home that night, cracking the eggs, and scrambling them on medium-high heat, just like I'd done with our Teflon pan countless times. It didn't take long before I recognized something was going wrong. The eggs smelled burnt, and the longer I cooked them the blacker the residue on the bottom of the pan became. While the eggs were mostly still liquid, I took the pan off the flame and poured the eggs down the sink.

That's when things got desperate.

Seeing how dirty the pan was, I figured I should clean it as soon as I could. I poured in some warm, soapy water and then set it aside for a moment to soak. Then, I took our only sponge and got to work.

I scrubbed.

And scrubbed.

And scrubbed.

I groaned.

I poured in more soap and hotter water.

I did everything I knew how to do—and the pan looked as if I'd not even tried.

So, I turned to Facebook. I put out a call into the ether: *I scrambled an egg in our brand-new steel pan, and now I've ruined it. Can't clean it—nothing works. What can I do?*

And, of course, this being the internet, the answer came back immediately: *Use steel wool, dummy.* I had to go out and buy it. But once I did, it was magic. The pan was back to glistening in a matter of seconds (and I felt completely ridiculous for the whole episode).

Story #2: One of the greatest mysteries of physics revolves around this question: what is light? In particular, what is its nature? What's it made of? Before the twentieth century, this question had vexed scientists for hundreds of years because experiments seemed to suggest opposite findings that obviously could not both be true: for many years, people assumed that light behaved as a wave because that's precisely what experiments showed; then, around the time Einstein came on the scene, new experiments seemed to indicate that light was not a wave but a collection of "particles"—tiny discrete units or packets. You can imagine how strange this seemed.

I won't go into the experimental details that seemed to buttress each argument, but I will highlight the fundamental contribution Einstein made to understanding the phenomenon of light. Scientists had assumed before he came on the scene that the resolution to the seeming contradiction would be that the evidence for one theory would overwhelm the other—one explanation would thrive and the other would shrivel. What happened instead was that Einstein led the way in discovering—and proving—something stranger and more beautiful than anyone could have supposed. Instead of one of the theories dying on the vine, Einstein helped show that they are *both* true, depending on our method of measurement and depending on the facet of light we are examining.[1]

Light is *both* a particle and a wave.

His finding suggests a fundamental paradox. The good news is that science discovered a solution to the puzzle; the bad news is that the solution bends the mind more than the question it seeks to answer. In some cases, light behaves one way, and in other circumstances, it behaves quite differently. Insofar as we understand, its behavior is not because of a weakness in measurement or a lack of comprehension but instead reflects a fundamental aspect of physical being—light has dual nature.

Is it wave or particle? It's both.

In this way, the whole situation is a little bit like the story of the blind people and the elephant—one felt a tail, one a tusk, one a foot, one a leg. Each person determined the nature of the elephant to be only the thing he or she had experienced, whereas in fact an elephant is all those things combined into one shared nature—which might be difficult to conceptualize if our observation were limited to any one aspect.

Out of this seemingly impossible fact about light has sprung the entire field of quantum physics, and the grandeur of the paradoxes and seemingly impossible situations that grow out of the field "makes reason stare."[2] For our purposes, however, the importance of this story is to note that there are instances in nature when we must consider an object to be of category X for some purposes but category Y for others. It turns out that this strange phenomenon (Einstein would eventually refer to some of the outgrowths of this idea as "spooky") is one of the unifying and fundamentally important laws of the universe.

Why do I share these two stories here? If we keep them in mind, I believe they help answer a question that confronts many people who think deeply about gaining spiritual knowledge: *How do we know the whole process described in previous chapters is not simply a loquacious defense of confirmation bias?*

Confirmation bias is a well-described psychological phenomenon—and unconscious mental trick—that helps us to safeguard and apparently defend our most cherished beliefs. If you can choose between believing thing A and thing B, and you have already come to believe that thing A is true, you will unconsciously prefer to recognize evidence supporting thing A and will similarly put aside evidence for thing B. This will happen consistently and unobtrusively such that you will not *feel* as though you are selectively weighing evidence. But this subtlety will deepen the impact of this selective process because you will believe you are considering things objectively and may even bristle at any suggestion otherwise.

Confirmation bias matters a lot because it is one piece of cognitive psychology that gets a lot of play nowadays, and when people of faith encounter the idea for the first time it can be devastating. Indeed, recognizing the role confirmation bias plays in our lives can be one of those paradigm-shifting moments when we say, "Oh goodness, has everything been a lie? Are all these things I believe (religious and not, for that matter) just stories I tell myself to make myself believe?"

But my experience is that the most devastating moment in the faith journey of many Saints is when they first *recognize* that confirmation bias informs what they've been doing. Having avoided changing the understanding they've held for so long, they finally arrive at a point, for whatever reason, where they feel compelled to take out every obscure detail they ever ignored and look those details in the eye all at once. That examination produces a doubly traumatic effect. First, because those details have not been dealt with previously, people suddenly feel overwhelmed by what they've learned: they've kept those things hidden so effectively that it is as if the new details are appearing all at once. But then, the effect of this blow is compounded by the sense that they have dealt with themselves dishonestly—whether they use the name or not, they look back and say, "Keeping that picture intact was nothing more than confirmation bias!"

And then the picture suddenly cracks, falling to the ground in shards. And what just the day before seemed such a solid testimony now lies in tatters.

In responding to this type of experience, then, we must consider the story beneath the story. On the one hand, the details of whatever bothers a believer are part of what's at play here. Beyond those details, however, lies a deeper question: is the whole project of sustaining faith nothing more than a conscious and willful version of confirmation bias? To put it differently—is the choice to believe one we make only because it's convenient? Or because it greases our family relationships? Or because the alternative is just too difficult to contemplate?

I don't believe this all amounts to a fatal flaw. First, we need to understand that a church—like light—boasts at least a dual nature. Yes, in some sense a church is a set of truth-claims, a collection of things we believe happened (e.g., the First Vision), ways we believe reality is (e.g., a spirit and a body together comprise a soul), and things we should and should not do. When we say we believe the Church is true, therefore, we are referencing a degree of confidence regarding how certain we are those things are true, even if we don't ar culate that. This type of understanding is reflected by the graphs shared throughout this book.

The thing is, that's only half the story—probably much less than half—because both the Church and the gospel are much more than a set of truth-claims. The Church is also the body of Christ— it is a collection not just of premises but of *people* trying to come together to form mini-Zions (and, we hope one day, a Zion to flood the world). By the same token, the gospel is not just premises but a transformative power; it's not just about believing X, Y, and Z are true but about allowing the power of grace to transform us—to shepherd us through a new birth in Christ.

This dual (or triple) nature matters a great deal: when we talk about church only as a collection of premises, the idea of confirmation bias makes sense. When we talk about church as a collection of people or as a repository for transformative grace, the whole idea of confirmation bias loses its resonance.

While I recognize the irony of saying, toward the end of a book filled with graphs and diagrams of confidence, that we need to be careful in applying only the rules of intellectual analysis to an evaluation of the Church's truth, it is nonetheless true. Because the Church is both particle and wave, tools that are useful in one context will not be in another. The sponge that cleans one pan beautifully will leave us howling in frustration if we try to use it to clean another.

We would cock a skeptical eyebrow if a friend said, "You should really stop paying so much attention to your spouse's virtues and focus on her/his vices. I'm afraid you're guilty of confirmation bias." And we would be right to be skeptical. In the same way, we should understand that if we fear jumping into the restored Christian life with both feet because it will expose us to allegations of confirmation bias, we may miss out on the sweet fruits that can come only from a lifetime of devoted discipleship. If I spend too much time dealing with historical accounts and the abstract details of theology, I can inadvertently pull myself away from the beating heart of restored Christianity. The entire reason the Church exists in the first place is to help us—by precept and covenant, in real communities with real people who have real needs—to become more like Jesus.

In this book we have encountered the Church as both wave and particle. On the one hand, we should be honest when we have intellectual concerns about the Church, and we should seek answers to our questions "by study and also by faith" (D&C 88:118). I believe intellectual questions about the Church have meaningful answers, and there are scores of books devoted to examining these ideas. Still, while being honest about these concerns, we should likewise take care to ensure that intellectual queries, no matter how honest or important, do not eclipse the real work of discipleship, which is more about action—loving God and loving our fellow humans—than it is about anything strictly intellectual. To continue faithfully in the pursuit of this kind of consecrated discipleship is not to fall victim to confirmation bias but instead to give ourselves over to the kind of consuming cause that makes life most meaningful.

Personal encounters with holy people have most effectively impressed this point upon me. I have met many good people, but I have been blessed every once in a great while to meet someone who impresses me as what I can describe only as "holy." Perhaps no one has personified this trait as beautifully for me as Emma Lou Thayne.

As described earlier, I knew Emma Lou relatively well growing up. What most sticks in my memory, however, is not her international peace work or even her captivating poetry—remarkable as both are—but rather that, during the last ten or so years of her life, when I would occasionally return home and get to see her, she could cup my face in her wizened, leathery hands and say in her deep, wise, almost guttural voice, "Oh, Tyler, what a treasure you are to the world—what a blessing." And I know she made everyone in her periphery feel just as treasured. It was hard not to think, when Emma Lou died, that the world had discernibly dimmed.

Emma Lou broke barriers and pushed envelopes, albeit mostly in a quiet way. She sat as the only woman on the *Deseret News* executive board[3]; she vigorously protested nuclear proliferation at a time when doing so was not popular in Utah; she wrote candidly about times she did not understand Church stances on this or that issue. She once quipped, when summing up her testimony of the Church's divine origins, "What it really had to with Joseph Smith and his vision I would never really know," while still affirming that she would be "cosmically orphaned" without the restored gospel. She championed conversations with and empathy toward the LGBTQ community when such a thing was virtually unheard of in her social, religious, and cultural circles. And she once memorably announced to her husband and daughters, right at the heart of her time as a mother, that she would be leaving for two weeks to go write poetry at a secluded retreat. She briefly left the family to figure out how to manage without her, disregarding the quizzical glances from neighbors.

The point of saying all of this is not that Emma Lou Thayne was perfect—certainly, she was not. Instead, I simply mean to point out this: she wore out her life pursuing a pathway of relentless discipleship and was sanctified as a result.[4] I benefited enormously from her light and was heartened to see that her funeral featured a crowd overflowing out of a large chapel, hallmarked by those who looked very out of place in a church—it was clear her embrace had drawn in people from all circles of life. Her life reminds me of the importance of Graph #7 in this chapter. What most mattered was not what she knew but who she had become and how that becoming lit, lifted, and blessed all who surrounded her.

Emma Lou's faith facilitated becoming a new being in Christ, a being in whom Christ's countenance shone and through whom Christ's gravitational love could easily operate.

Faith is not ultimately about accepting cognitive premises. Rather, it is the love that kept the prodigal son's father eagerly scanning the horizon and the fire that burned under the father's feet as he ran to embrace his son (see Luke 15:11–32); it is the bravery that allowed the Anti-Nephi-Lehies to bury their weapons and willingly give their lives rather than take up arms again (see Alma 24);

it is the grit that kept Lehi's few walking through the mists of darkness only to fall down at the tree of light (see 1 Nephi 8); it is the suspicion that brought Mary, bereft, to Jesus's empty tomb, and the hunch that bore Peter and John on their sprint to that same sepulcher (see John 20:1–18); it is the buoyancy that kept Peter afloat, atop the churning waters; it is the humility that brought the boy Joseph to his knees in the sacred grove; it is the uncertain drive that allows a young missionary to attempt to be the Lord's emissary; it is the only force in heaven or earth that can work together with the enabling power of the Savior's Atonement to allow us to become like Christ.

A DISCIPLESHIP THAT BLESSES THE WORLD

Beyond the miraculous individual transformation that faith promises, there lies an even greater call. If we do not turn our attention to this final reason for religion, we fail to examine religion's most vital and probing purpose.

Sometimes in Church culture, we are prone to define our religious identity by a series of things we should and should not do. This list is familiar to all Church members, and even to many people who are not members of our faith. Indeed, if you were to ask a random woman on the street what she knows about members of The Church of Jesus Christ of Latter-day Saints, she might very well respond, "Members of that church don't drink, don't smoke, don't have sex, and I've even heard they wear funny underwear." Though perhaps not as obvious to outsiders, we would add to this list praying multiple times a day, reading scriptures regularly, fasting monthly, listening to and studying addresses from modern-day prophets and apostles, and so on.

That this list is so widely known—and that it is arguably the easiest way to recognize a member of our Church—gladdens me

and concerns me. It gladdens me because in many cases these religious habits cut against the cultural current and really do make
us a "peculiar people" (1 Peter 2:9). The fact that we take this list
seriously speaks highly of us.

Even so, there is a danger lurking behind this well-known list,
because many of the things for which we are most known concern what I might call "inward-facing discipleship." These are commandments that concern what we eat, what we drink, what we
wear, what words we use, what we read, what we listen to, and how
we spend our time. Again, I endorse this list. The inner life of a
restored Christian disciple matters. And I believe that following the
precepts of inward-facing discipleship prepares us for the work of
gathering Israel and building Zion.

And yet, the inner life of a disciple is a necessary but insufficient
work. While necessary, these things must finally be a means, not an
end. Or, at least if they do form an end, that end is incomplete and
even dangerous if left unalloyed by a broader religious goal.

The problem with inward-facing discipleship—at least when
it comes to consume a person's religious life—is that without
leavening by a broader, other-centered impulse, it can become
brittle, self-centered, narrow-minded, and, in some extreme cases,
self-righteous or hypocritical. Indeed, it is neither exaggeration nor
spin to observe that the Savior's harshest rebukes came not to the
adulterous or even the greedy but to overtly religious people who
had allowed their version of inward-facing discipleship to eclipse
the weightier matters of the law.

Remember: when Jesus was asked which were the greatest
commandments, He said they were to love God and to love our
fellow men (see Matthew 22:34–40).

It follows that the precepts of inward-facing discipleship mel-
low, teach, calm, and prepare us so that we can then embark on

the collective mission of building Zion. In other words, we are reminded that the "inward-facing" acts of discipleship are not, in fact, inward-facing at all—or at least if we believe they face us only in that direction, this misunderstanding demonstrates that we have misunderstood their purpose. After all, the whole point of daily devotional practices is to turn us toward God, and when we do so, He will inevitably turn us toward those who need our help, and most especially to those at the margins, the vulnerable, and the poor.

I have been struck during the prophetic ministry of President Russell M. Nelson by the consistency with which he has addressed the gathering of Israel. This insistence is noteworthy in part because that gathering necessarily focuses us outside the borders of the Church—his talks on this subject elevate and broaden our gaze.

Of course, we are called to perfect the Saints. And ministering to our own will always constitute one of discipleship's most important commandments and covenants. Nevertheless, we cannot allow the reach of our stewardship to extend only to the boundaries of our wards and stakes. The scriptures shout from their literary rooftops this fundamental truth: the Lord has called our relatively small worldwide band of restored Christian disciples to bless the whole world. Ultimately, each of us has been given a unique stewardship, and one day we will be called to account for how we have dispensed it.

The restored gospel offers a meaningful, profound, and holistic understanding of our identity, divinity, destiny, and purpose. This knowledge should serve as a balm to our own secret wounds and as a light when we find ourselves in darkness. But that alone is not the call of discipleship. No, Jesus calls us to venture forth into a weary and suffering world. He invites us to live a life of inward-facing discipleship to equip us with the love, resilience, health, perspective, organizational wherewithal, and grit to become a force for good in the world.

WALKING THE COVENANT PATH

In this regard, I have been brought recently to think deeply about President Nelson's invitation to "keep on the covenant path."[5] This phrase has been a hallmark of his ministry. Yet, sometimes I feel that we often don't give much thought to what it means. Of course, in one sense we might envision walking the covenant path to simply mean receiving each necessary ordinance: baptism, confirmation, conferral of the priesthood for men, receipt of the temple endowment, and, eventually, sealing. I do not question the value of the ordinances, but I believe we are called to understand this road more deeply. It was then-Elder Oaks who warned us against envisioning life as a series of needed celestial bank deposits. He reminded us that living the gospel life is not just about what we do—it is about who we become.[6]

Similarly, President Nelson recently taught in general conference:

Overcoming the world is not an event that happens in a day or two. It happens over a lifetime as we repeatedly embrace the doctrine of Christ. We cultivate faith in Jesus Christ by repenting daily and keeping covenants that endow us with power. We stay on the covenant path and are blessed with spiritual strength, personal revelation, increasing faith, and the ministering of angels. . . .

As we strive to live the higher laws of Jesus Christ, our hearts and our very natures begin to change. The Savior lifts us above the pull of this fallen world by blessing us with greater charity, humility, generosity, kindness, self-discipline, peace, and *rest*.[7]

We must then ask, *If walking the covenant path is the very point of our lives, what kind of people are those covenants inviting us to become?* President Nelson hints at the answer to this above, but let's explore in more depth what specific scriptural accounts say about the direction and effect of this transformation. If we agree that the steps along the covenant path are meant as transformative spiritual experiences, what is the resulting metamorphosis supposed to look like? We could analyze all ordinances under this rubric, but for our purpose's we'll consider just two: our first covenant—baptism—and the covenants we make when we receive the endowment.

We often speak of our baptismal covenants as if they are summarized in the sacrament prayers, but that is nowhere stated explicitly in scripture. Instead, for an explanation of what it means to be baptized, I turn to two major verses from Restoration scripture. The first is Doctrine and Covenants 20:37, which reads, "All those who humble themselves before God, and desire to be baptized, and come forth with broken hearts and contrite spirits, and witness before the church that they have truly repented of all their sins, and are willing to take upon them the name of Jesus Christ, having a determination to serve Him to the end, and truly manifest by their works that they have received of the Spirit of Christ unto the remission of their sins, shall be received by baptism into his church." Importantly, this verse talks mostly about what we must do to prepare to be baptized and what that state of readiness looks like. In terms of what baptism actually entails, however, it says only that we must have a "determination to serve [God] to the end." For a description of what that service looks like, we turn to Mosiah 18.

Here, as discussed earlier, Alma reminds his listeners that they will know they are ready to be baptized if they are ready to mourn with those who mourn and comfort those who stand in need of comfort and to stand as God's witnesses (see Mosiah 18:9). In other words, in Alma's formulation, the covenants we make at the time of baptism consist of two main promises: a commitment to being a witness for God in the world and a willingness to weave oneself into a covenant community in Christ. Being baptized consists of a promise to bind ourselves in covenantal empathy to those around us. We have discussed in great detail in previous chapters what the resulting communities can look like and what our commitment to those we love within them entails.

And that brings us to the Restoration's crowning covenants: those we make in the temple. In previous eras, we did not speak openly about temple covenants outside the temple, but the Church has recently clarified that we are welcome to speak about them reverently and respectfully,[8] and that is what I will endeavor to do here.

In effect, we make five main covenants when we enter the temple (this summary of our covenants in the endowment is quoted from the Church Handbook, which is publicly available online):

- To live the law of sacrifice;
- To live the law of obedience;
- To live the law of the gospel;
- To live the law of chastity;
- And to live the law of consecration.

For this discussion, I would like to turn our attention to two of the covenants—the law of sacrifice and the law of consecration. These two covenants join together to invite us to change the paradigm of our lives. To understand why, we need to review a bit of history.

Members of the Church in the 1830s were (briefly, and often more in theory than in practice) asked to legally deed all they owned to the Church. Under this framework, the bishop would collect the donations into a "storehouse." Goods from that collection would then be used to bless the poor and provide for the community. Individual members, now without anything at all, would then meet with the bishop, and together they would determine a just "stewardship" for the coming year. The bishop would then make that member and the member's family stewards over the resources they had agreed upon. Members would take that stewardship and do their best with it. After a year, they would meet with the bishop again to give an accounting of how they and their families had stewarded the goods put under their care. This arrangement was alternately known as the "law of consecration" or the "law of the Lord," and was founded on the principle of sacrifice. Thus, though we speak of it rarely, this theoretical precedent may be seen as the historical basis for two of the five main temple covenants.

Of course, communities based on the law of consecration as a governing financial system never worked in the 1830s and was of very limited use later. It came into operation briefly in a few select communities when the Saints moved out West, but the human limitations of the Saints prevented it from ever blossoming into the blessed sociality described, for example, in 4 Nephi. As an actual economic order, it has not existed in many years.

And yet, when we go to the temple, we covenant to live the law of sacrifice and the law of consecration—and thus, though the formal economic order was long ago done away, the law that supported it remains robustly in effect. In the temple, we covenant to consecrate all with which the Lord has blessed us to build up God's kingdom and to work toward Zion.

As I've grown older, I have come to appreciate more and more the importance of these covenants. In the first place, living the law of consecration invites us to shift the defining paradigm of our lives from ownership to stewardship. For me, this shift has been definitional. I still struggle to get it right, but it redefines the way I view everything I have. In a world of ownership, acquisition is my focus and the measure of my worth and, if I am not careful, I can easily become entitled, bitter, and selfish.

But in a world of stewardship, I am awed at the blessings heaven has showered down upon me and anxious to use them to bless and to build. Because I do not "own" anything, I have no more claim on my time, money, and resources than anyone else, and I am constantly on the lookout for ways to use my abundance to lift the poor and help the needy. For those of us who live in the most temporally prosperous era in world history, this recognition—that all that we have does not actually belong to us, but is given as a stewardship—becomes weighty and vital: can I ever possibly do enough to adequately discharge the stewardship that has been granted to me? The law of consecration in this light is an insistent, incessant reminder that even if I wear out the rest of my life in service, I will still fall far short of my full potential to do good.

Paradoxically, though, even as our attempts to use our stewardship to bless the world grow, we usually find our gratitude growing commensurately. Freed from the incessant nagging of acquisitiveness, we can instead find beauty in sunrises, bird songs, smiles, hugs, and beautiful music. Our abundance grows, even as we try to give it away.

Beyond these blessings of living a life of general stewardship, we are called in the temple endowment to very specifically consecrate ourselves to building the Church and Zion. Because we no longer deed all we have to the Church, it is left to us to determine how to discharge our consecration. I would like to think about each of these covenants—to build the Church, and to build Zion—in turn.

I think we often misunderstand what it might mean to build "the Church," because we often narrow unnecessarily what is meant by "the Church." It is true that in one sense "the Church" is a theoretical thing defined by a certain ecclesiology, history, and authority. But this theoretical church model doesn't really need our building. Instead, when I covenant to consecrate to "build the Church," I am effectively covenanting to build the people I see around me on Sunday.

These people—in all their imperfections—are "the Church." So, those of us who have been to the temple have covenanted to consecrate all that we have and are to building the people who sit in the pews with us each Sabbath—and those who are our neighbors, whether they attend church or not. And what a beautiful promise that is. After all, while not everyone lives in a nuclear family, everyone can belong to a branch or ward. In Elder Gerrit W. Gong's words, "We can come by covenant to belong with God and a community of faithful believers and receive the blessings promised in the doctrine of Christ—now."[9]

And in this sense, by dedicating our lives to our covenant Christian communities, we even make the Church more "true." It becomes more "true" in the sense that by keeping both our baptismal and our temple covenants, we are "true" to each other, and in being true to each other we weave together a social fabric that, in its best iterations, provides refuge for the weary and respite to the faint. We do not routinely think of the Church's "truth" as hinging on the way we treat and support each other in our covenant Christian communities, but the large majority of the time we spend doing Church things, we spend within the walls of our own local chapels. In the final analysis, little that is "true" about the Church will feel like it matters if we are not true to one another.

And that all brings us, finally, to the last covenantal call: to build Zion. Zion can be defined in many ways, but I like to think of it like this: the call to build Zion is, quite simply, our divine mandate to make the world a better place. When you speak well of a colleague at work, you are building Zion. When you work to fight against racism, you are building Zion. When you put out into the world edifying art or music, you are building Zion. When you provide professional counseling to a teen in crisis, you are building Zion. When you teach French in a troubled high school, you are building Zion. When you do research that advances medical cures, you are building Zion. When you offer a friend a kind word or a needed smile, you are building Zion. If you win an election and go on to bring better resources to the poor, you are building Zion. When you work hard to be CEO, or a nanny, or chairwoman of the board, or president of the PTA, or a leader in tech or industry, or a lawyer fighting for civil rights, or an attorney working to document the undocumented, or a neighbor bringing soup to the homeless, or a doctor bringing care to the dying, or whatever good and luminous thing you may one day become—so long as you are leveraging your many gifts to build and better the children of our heavenly parents, you are building Zion.

We come as well to one of the temple's most potent symbols. At the center of both the endowment and the sealing rooms sits a simple altar—but that altar represents what the restored Christian life demands of us. Christ is not asking for us to putter around at the edges of our lives. He is not offering a self-help course or a few "life hacks" to make us feel more fulfilled. It just doesn't work like that—and each of the ordinances along the covenant path emphasizes that truth. In baptism, our old selves die, and we are born as new creatures in Christ; in the temple, we are asked to place on that altar not the offering of a sacrificial animal, as in the times of ancient Israel, but rather a broken heart and a contrite spirit. We are asked to subjugate every part of ourselves to the cause of Christ—because it is not a matter of giving this or that part of ourselves but instead a matter of those very selves being laid on the altar, consecrated to the ministerial life to which we are called.

It is considering all the foregoing that I think of my temple garments. I wear my garments for many reasons, but chief among them is that as the clothing closest to my skin and the thing that virtually never leaves my side, my garments remind me that my covenant to consecrate is total and ever-binding. Whether my service is to my family, my ward, or the wider world, I am to wear out my life in serving, building, and blessing.

In making my family, my ward, and the world better.

Walking the covenant path is not just checking off a list of required ordinances. It is, instead, a call to *become a certain kind of person*, and the scriptures are very specific about what that kind of person looks like and what that kind of person does. While we forever remain imperfect—individually and collectively—to the degree we fail to live up to our promise to relentlessly mend, heal, lift, buoy, build, and better the world, we are neglecting the charge that comprises the beating heart of covenant Christian discipleship.

And with that realization, we begin to grasp perhaps the most foundational paradox underlying the entire premise of this book. Much of what we have here discussed has been an explanation of what it means to believe and doubt, to have faith and know. I have provided extensive graphs of the processes we each might experience. But even as I do so, I fear that this discussion may exacerbate a cultural quirk to which we are already too susceptible—namely, the idea that the purpose of religion is to demonstrate the superiority of our particular set of historical and theological claims.

We sometimes behave as if we think we will be greeted upon dying with a multiple-choice test, and that our answers to that exam form the essence of our discipleship. I wish to push back firmly on this unspoken cultural assumption.

It instead seems to me much more likely and much more scriptural that when we die, we will simply be asked by the Lord, "Considering all I gave you—materially and spiritually—what did you do to show your love for Me by blessing the world?" In this formulation, a correct sense of divine identity and destiny becomes not a reason for theological bragging but instead a blessed grounding in the universe's most fundamental truth—our knowledge of our identity catalyzes an instinct to make peace, bring hope, and enable healing throughout the world.

Herein we come to understand that we must build Zion precisely so that Israel has a place to gather. Under this understanding, it is not surprising that President Nelson has recently invited us to "lead out in abandoning attitudes and actions of prejudice"[10]— after all, what could be more antithetical to the gathering of Israel than sorting people into hierarchical buckets based on the amount of melanin in their skin?

G. K. Chesterton once wrote allegorically of a man who was so obsessed with himself that he had stopped recognizing the reality of the world around him. In his allegory, the point of religion and theology is to pull us out of our self-contained world and to really see the reality of the beings around us for the first time. As Chesterton wrote, when the man finally escapes his narcissism, he finds himself "under a freer sky, and in a street full of splendid strangers."[11]

I hope that our doubts about the veracity of this or that historical or theological claim will eventually fade, not so much because we have arrived at a state of unquestioning certainty—which is often impossible and sometimes undesirable—but instead because the absolute certainty of truth-claims fades in significance when seen against the pressing need to feed the hungry, comfort the sad, welcome the refugee, and bind up the wounds of the hurting.

Let us be faithful.

Let us make our acts of personal devotion deep and true.

And then, let us go forth into a world awash in suffering, demonstrating that our claim to fame as a religion should not be the drinks we drink (or don't) or the things we read, but the ways that the world is better for our being there.

And with this call ringing in our ears, we return, one final time, to Esperanza.

When last we left her, she found herself under a lightless sky, with clouds obscuring the stars. Those clouds symbolized a dark night of the soul: the scriptures, prayer, and church attendance that had brought her succor during the first few years after her conversion somehow turned suddenly empty—without life or light.

Let's suppose that things did not soon grow any easier. Esperanza is a woman of her word, and since she meant what she said when she was baptized, we see her continuing going to church, reading her scriptures, and saying her prayers—but for weeks that turn into months it's not clear that her heart is in it. It's not that she isn't trying. She just feels as though she's knocking at the heavenly door and finding no one is there.

What's more, questions continue to plague her—about her place in the Church as a woman, about polygamy, about the racial priesthood restriction, about it all. She wonders if her life is a lie. She senses that what she is doing should mean more to her than it does.

Yet she persists.

Then one morning, she is walking to church, downtown in the big city where she lives. She's running late, her pace is quick, and she's frustrated to see that, as is so often the case, men who are begging for money and food line the sidewalk a few blocks away from the chapel. As she has done every Sunday for the years she has lived there, she winds her way between their outstretched legs and is about to hurry off to sacrament meeting, when a gleam catches her eye—light, it turns out, reflected from a pin on the last man's baseball cap.

Despite herself, before she even knows what she is doing, she turns to look at the flash, and a man with sallow skin and pouches resting beneath both eyes looks up at her, holding weathered hands out in a cupping shape, asking for change.

In that moment, *the thing* happens again: it is as though her very heavy heart breaks open inside her, and somehow, in a way she will try for the rest of her life to describe or explain, the man's countenance is suddenly illuminated, and she locks eyes with him—his are veined and yellowing—and sees in him something she has never seen in any person, anywhere, before.

And then she has stretched out her hands—she feels the callouses that pad his fingers as she helps him to his feet. She sees he is bent with age and has difficulty walking, so she steadies him, walks him to the restaurant in the next building, and pays for his food, buying him enough for that meal and the next. She sits with him while he eats. And then, forty-five minutes later as she leaves, she looks at him with an emotion sprung up from nowhere, with a sincerity flowing from some secret inner fountain.

She looks around despite herself as she leaves the restaurant— and knows she just tasted something like charity, and everything around her is somehow lighter for her having been there.

Now hopelessly late for church, she finally walks into the chapel as they are wrapping up the closing hymn. She sits in the pew and finds the words forming on her lips before she has recognized the song:

> *Then in a moment to my view*
> *The stranger started from disguise.*
> *The tokens in his hands I knew;*
> *The Savior stood before mine eyes.*
> *He spake, and my poor name he named,*
> *"Of me thou hast not been ashamed.*

These deeds shall thy memorial be;
Fear not, thou didst them unto me. "[12]

And then, as the final strains of the chorus wash over her, she finds a light and warmth enveloping her in a manner so comprehensive and comfortable she is sure visible light must be streaming from somewhere, but finds only the drab yellow chapel walls in every direction. Her questions have not vanished—they persist, and some will never go away—but she blinks tears from her eyes and looks around at a chapel full of people who have loved her as she has loved them over the past three years, and it is suddenly not that the questions don't matter, but just that everyone around her—the man begging, the chorister, the child in front of her, the woman to the side—matter so much more.

Her believing is fired not by intellectual inquiry, but by belonging and becoming beloved.

Her believing is simply that: love.

AFTERWORD

HEARING
THE MUSIC AGAIN

I was twenty-one and a college sophomore when I first heard the BYU Singers' rendition of Edward Elgar's "Lux Aeterna." Originally composed in 1899, "Lux Aeterna" was written as one of fourteen orchestral pieces together called the Enigma Variations. Elgar named the set "Enigma" because all fourteen apparently trace themselves back to a single initial melody whose identity has never been definitively demonstrated. Each variation is dedicated to one of Elgar's friends or loved ones, and the ninth is dedicated to Augustus Jaeger, Elgar's friendly critic with London publishing house Novello & Co.

Elgar reported that, during a time of great despair—when he was nearly ready to give up composing—Jaeger insisted he continue and referred him to the second movement of Ludwig van Beethoven's eighth sonata, commonly known as Sonata Pathétique, for inspiration. Thus, the ninth variation hearkens back to that melody, in addition to the above-described mystery one, and is called "Nimrod" in an allusion to the Old Testament hunter from Genesis 10 (Jaeger is "hunter" in German). The song has since become immensely popular internationally, having been recorded multiple times. You might want to Google it to listen while you read this chapter.

Of course, I knew none of that history when I first heard the song, which was later arranged for eight voices and given Latin lyrics, translated below:

> *May light eternal shine upon them,*
> *O Lord, with Thy Saints forever,*
> *for Thou art kind.*
> *Eternal rest*
> *give to them, O Lord,*
> *and let perpetual light shine upon them.*

What I knew immediately the first time I heard the song, however, was that I would never be the same. The song starts on a single, plaintive F held first by the altos and then the sopranos for more than two full bars. Soon the remaining parts join in, and the choir falls into a lilting, almost hypnotic recitation that lasts about four pages, all before the parts suddenly split into a wider and resplendent vocal palette that climaxes in a series of chords of such devastating beauty that the first time I heard them I sat staring long after the song had ended, straining my ears to hear any echo of the notes still hanging in the air.

During that sophomore year, I must have listened to the song hundreds of times. I had never been party to such beauty before, and I found myself transfixed. It was as if I had found beauty itself for the first time and couldn't get enough—as if listening to the song endlessly might open to me the secret that allowed that collection of notes to burrow so deeply into my soul and leave my heart both singing and weeping.

I had sung in choirs in high school, but I largely worked my way through college—between demanding studies and steady part-time jobs, singing in choirs had to go. It was perhaps ironic, then, that this period was when I first really listened to music. The same CD that featured "Lux Aeterna" also showcased Morten Lauridsen's "O Nata Lux" and Eric Whitacre's incomparable "When David Heard That Absalom Was Slain." These songs—and many, many others—became for me an anchor and respite. Discovering them was like happening on a new national park, unlike any I'd ever before visited. I set about acquainting myself with its every canyon and peak, its every tree and stream, and in so doing found a new type of holy ground, one to which I would return endlessly over the subsequent years.

Since then, any time I have sought refuge, Elgar and his friends have been there. It is no exaggeration to say in this context that the spring of 2019 featured one of my life's highlights—singing "Lux Aeterna," surrounded by friends who are also in my choir, with the notes echoing resplendently off the stone walls of the Santa Clara Mission Cathedral in northern California. Learning vocal music, as much as I love it, does not come particularly easily to me. And so, in preparation for our performance, I spent hours at a piano with my pencil in hand and "Lux" in front of me, rehearsing the notes again and again and again. By the time our lone concert came in April, the notes were tattooed in my DNA, and I sank into the flow of the choir, the melodies flowing from me as easily as prayer.

It was a moment never to be forgotten.

Perhaps the above helps explain why Wilford W. Andersen's 2015 address in general conference struck me so deeply and has stuck with me ever since. Elder Neil L. Andersen recounted a story of a young doctor working on a Navajo reservation. One day, an older Native American man came into the doctor's emergency room looking for help. When the doctor entered the man's room, the man sat there, silent, even after the doctor asked him repeatedly what was wrong. Finally, and without responding directly to the doctor's questions, the old man asked the doctor, "Do you dance?" The doctor recognized that the older man may have been a traditional medicine man who would be accustomed to healing via song and dance. Accordingly, the doctor replied, "I don't dance. Do you dance?" When the medicine man nodded in affirmation, the young doctor asked, "Could you teach me to dance?" And then came the medicine man's reply: "I can teach you to dance, but you have to hear the music."

Elder Andersen goes on to compare the "music" of the gospel to the sweet fruits of the Spirit that are a source of our motivation to live gospel standards. He reminds us that the discipline required to perform the "dance steps" will always matter but says it can become grating, wearying, and even nonsensical if the dance steps are forced of their own accord rather than arising organically as a joyful response to the gospel's heavenly music.[1]

I have often pondered this imagery in the context of my experience falling in love with "Lux Aeterna," "O Nata Lux," and "When David Heard That Absalom Was Slain." In the years since first hearing these songs, there have been periods—some short, some long—when that music has been a lifeline to the divine. When all around me seemed frustrating, confusing, or strange, I knew I could reliably queue that song, extinguish the lights, and lie there in the darkness, allowing the waves of sound to crash over me, washing me in heavenly light.

I have wondered sometimes, however: *What if one day I awoke and found myself deaf to the music?* What if, one morning, with a heart weighed down with sorrow, I turned on the song, saw the seconds ticking by on the digital counter, but somehow heard only silence? I can imagine myself checking the speakers, figuring that whatever was wrong would be an easy fix, only to find over time that, in fact, no music would come. I would grow frantic, hopeless—desperately clawing my memory, looking for a trace of the sound.

Or, even worse: what if I one day pressed play and, even after checking and rechecking to reassure myself that I really was listening to Elgar's "Nimrod," found that the notes had somehow terribly rearranged themselves into a cacophony, stripped of beauty and harmony, filled instead with dissonance and chaos?

I'd be devastated.

This analogy is my own (springing, to a degree, from Elder Andersen's), but it holds true to stories I have heard from many friends with whom I've talked and counseled over the years. More than one former believer has pled with me, in effect, *I used to hear the music, and it sang to me, transported me, healed me—but I just can't hear it anymore. God is unreachable and the Church no longer makes sense.*

Please, someone, teach me how to hear the music again.

In their plaintive cries, I'm reminded of Alma, who asked, "If ye have experienced a change of heart, and if ye have felt to sing the song of redeeming love, I would ask, can ye feel so now?" (Alma 5:26). There are few things more probing than the cries of one who no longer can.

For all the logic and graphs in this book, for all the sources I've quoted and the analyses I've offered, I end here on something of a personal note:

I believe in resurrection.

Admittedly, I have a hard time understanding how our physical bodies will again assume a physiologically sound form. I have also noted that faith changes, and when it does, it is fruitless to imagine it can ever go back to what it was before. Still, though, I believe our bodies and spirits will be united and that, if we do our imperfect but sincere and consistent best, we will be able to live forever, perfect in God's presence. And even here on earth, I believe in spiritual rebirth. I believe in Paul and in Alma, in the reality of the prodigal son. And, no less miraculous, I believe that even after a dark night of the soul, through the tenacity of faith and the reality of Christ's grace, belief can be reborn into something new and beautiful, over and over and over again.

As a spiritually serious teen, I traveled one year to visit the Sacred Grove—and I seized on that opportunity to "gain a testimony." I was sure no young person could have been more earnest or wholehearted than I was—when I separated myself from my family that spring morning and began praying, I half expected my own angelic visitation. I set about praying and hoping and waiting and listening for an hour—but exactly *nothing* happened. I muttered to myself on the way out, "Well, I don't know what all that was about."

A few months later, my teenage mind had long ago forgotten about that morning in the grove. One Sunday, heading home from church, my dad asked me to prepare a home teaching lesson—we would be sharing Joseph Smith's First Vision (the 1838 version). I sat on the couch in our front room, facing the bay window and read about Joseph's confusion and desire to know which church was right.

Then, I arrived at "I saw a pillar of light, exactly over my head. . . ."

And that thing happened.

In the twenty-five years or so since, I have entirely failed at describing my experience that morning. It was as if all light, and everything sweet and beautiful, coalesced at a focal point inside of me. I had no sense then what I was experiencing, and I would never develop words to say what it meant or what it was—but in the moments following that unbidden experience I felt like I could say, "I know."

And yet.

Since that time, all simplicity has vanished. About Joseph Smith, especially, the historical record has very much muddied the waters. Joseph recounted the First Vision again and again over many years, and the versions differ in important aspects. The characteristics I first thought defined the vision weren't even always emphasized—the vision meant many things to many people over decades. Similarly, the rest of Joseph's life was often hardly what anyone would draw up for the life of the Restoration's inaugural prophet. Frankly, I find many things he did puzzling, discomfiting, and sometimes genuinely concerning.

And even beyond Joseph Smith, the rest of what we believe has proven endlessly messy and never uncomplicated. Our early history is littered with colorful characters, many of them apostles and prophets. And even our modern discourse and policies have aroused in me emotions as strong and complex as fury, sadness, frustration, confusion, and bewilderment. My nights spent weeping with those I love within the Church have been more numerous that I would have wished or supposed.

So why am I still here?

Sometimes I imagine myself along Lehi's and Nephi's proverbial narrow path, clinging to the iron rod. I now visualize that experience from my teen years like a glimpse of the tree and its radiant fruit when both remained yet far off. Long since, the mists of darkness have wrapped their tendrils around me, shrouding me in obsidian and leaving me reliant on the rod to make my way toward the tree.

Yet, every so often, even if the mists have not yet cleared, some sounds make their tenuous but insistent way through the fog. Carried on the wind, from the direction of those luminous branches, I feel the heavenly music—soft but strong—pulsing toward my heart and ears. I hear it when I am wrapped in the goodness of a community that lifts and cares for me; when I sense the divinity underlying the functioning of my body; when I feel covenants keeping me connected in love to God and those around me; when an ineloquent friend's blessing words take on heavenly luster; when, teaching, I glimpse a truth from God; when I sense divine whispers within the words of a prophet; when I divine the temple's heavenly echoes; when a patient approaches dying and I sense the veil fluttering nearby.

None of these experiences is about "knowing" any more than a sunrise is about doing algebra, but each of them is a whisper, an echo, a memory—a ripple undulating across the eternal sea. One of the restored gospel's most magnificent proposals is this: beyond the noise and chaos that too often fills our lives shimmers a celestial singing that would stun us if we but had ears to hear. I do not—yet—but I catch just enough of those heavenly echoes to make me suspicious that that reality is *actually* there. And so, though the more I know the less I *know*, I still capture floating toward me through the darkness what Emma Lou Thayne called that "insistent, confounding, so help me sacred singing."[2] And when I hear it:

I believe.

At the end of the day, there is something genuinely anachronistic about living the gospel of the restored Church of Jesus Christ. Where modern life zips from hyperlink to hyperlink, discipleship requires sustained devotion to fixed principles over a lifetime. The process of becoming people who evoke Christ and have His image demands from us belief, faith, and diligence that belie the modern ethos of satisfaction on demand.

The true glory of the gospel lies beyond the fairy tale some of us have concocted about what restored Christianity should be. Indeed, I would say that the fairy tale was simply that: a mirage. We ought never to have expected a church populated or led by the perfect, nor an unfurling of a kingdom immune from the difficulties and sins that are the lot of all humans. The gospel does not shine because it is a fairy tale—it shines because once we push past the fairy tale, we find it offers deep, substantive, and enduring succor. The *real* gospel is what remains when the fairy tale has fallen away.

The gospel matters so much because in an age of isolation, it binds us into communities; in an untethered time, it bonds us by covenant to God and each other; in an age of ambiguity, it offers meaning; in an age of desperation, it offers hope; and in an age of the echoing, empty, and careless cosmos, it offers us an empathic, invested, omniscient Heavenly Father and Mother whose hearts beat in sympathy with ours.

I believe that the rebirth of our belief is something worth waiting for.

This is so even if, like Mother Teresa, we sometimes feel God has grown silent, or even if, like Mary, we feel we have watched the object of our belief die. I don't know all the reasons our belief sometimes goes silent, even at times when we are doing our diligent best to live as Christian disciples. I believe, however, that such times demand the best of us: even in the silence, God asks us to continue to be faithful—to hope when we are past hope, to believe in the face of what seem like valid reasons to question our belief. It is then that we must rely on what Elder Jeffrey R. Holland called "the yearning, burning commitment of the soul"[3] to bring us safely to the farther shore.

And why should we persist in the face of such silence? Because the world is bereft without music, and nothing so blesses the silence of the soul as the reawakening of the songs we most deeply long to sing. And, paradoxically, because when we labor to bind ourselves together in empathy and to draw closer to God together, even when we no longer hear the music, we find that that very act creates a beauty and harmony all its own.

ACKNOWLEDGMENTS

This manuscript has now been in the works for many years. Whatever good it does owes largely to the love and care lavished on it by many friends. At the risk of leaving some contributors unnamed, I would like to specifically thank the following:

- Jana Riess, who received the manuscript when it was in a much-less-fully-formed state; she loved the book enough to give me (sometimes painfully) candid feedback. Her pushing me to reach further resulted in what I now believe to be the book's finest sections.
- Rachel Ruekert, who read the manuscript as a second editor. While the book was in much fuller form by the time she saw it, she offered much-needed encouragement and also recommended important grace note suggestions that have helped round the manuscript into final form.
- Richard Price and Peter Wilson, whose incisive commentary and deep thinking have greatly improved both the reasoning and the prose.

ACKNOWLEDGMENTS

- Andy Griffin, whose graphs and illustrations probably make whole pages of my writing superfluous, and whose great care in creating those same figures reflects the passion he pours into everything he does.
- Calvin Burke and Eliza Wells, both of whom I met as college students, and both of whom offered much-needed deep thinking—I especially thank both of them for helping me to think about how the book would sound to members of marginalized communities.
- Nicholas Welch, for being a copy editor extraordinaire and a dear friend.
- Patrick Mason, Kristine Haglund, Paul Reeve, JB Haws, and Steve Harper—all of whom are much more experienced writers and each of whom read part or all of the manuscript and offered suggestions for improving it.
- Sunny Stimmler, who for decades has been a partner in thinking and writing about things that really matter, and who kindly offers time she doesn't really have.
- Russell Hancock, whose preaching and writing on some of these subjects is repeatedly cited but whose influence on my thinking runs both more broadly and deeply than those few citations acknowledge.
- Becca Warthen consistently insists I make things "half as long," and generally pushes me to think, write, and love on a higher plane. The marginalized and disconsolate have no more consistent friend.
- And finally, Norm and Julie Johnson, for teaching me consistently that the gospel is a big tent where all people should find love, and for teaching me that writing is a craft worth honing.

There are others who have likewise affected my thinking and writing. I hope they will not take their inadvertent omission from this list as any slight of their contributions—to all of these I am deeply grateful.

Nonetheless, this work is, finally, my own in content and tone.

Tyler Johnson

NOTES

CHAPTER 1: OUR BRAVE NEW WORLD

1. Eliza R. Snow, "My Father in Heaven," Oct. 1845, *Times and Seasons* (Nauvoo, IL), Nov. 15, 1845, vol. 6, no. 17.
2. For evidence from within our own faith tradition, see Jana Reiss, *The Next Mormons: How Millennials Are Changing the LDS Church* (Oxford University Press, 2019).
3. In this brief section I'll largely address specifics from the United States, but the trends in the United States reflect the broad contours in much of the rest of the world and the overall direction in the world as a whole.
4. "Public Trust in Government: 1958–2022," Pew Research Center, June 6, 2022, https://www.pewresearch.org/politics/2022/06/06/public-trust-in-government-1958-2022/. Note: One could argue that the change here reflects the fact that we are listening to a broader array of voices than we were sixty years ago, and that African American citizens, for instance, would likely not have expressed trust in a government that still supported the Jim Crow

regime in many places. Still, even among those who were being asked sixty years ago, the sense of trust has diminished significantly.

5. Art Swift, "Americans' Trust in Mass Media Sinks to New Low," Gallup, September 14, 2016, https://news.gallup.com/poll/195542/americans -trust-mass-media-sinks-new-low.aspx.

6. American Friends Service Committee, *Speak Truth to Power: A Quaker Search for an Alternative to Violence* (American Friends Service Committee, 1955).

7. Mike Conway, "The origins of the all-powerful news anchor," *The Conversation*, February 25, 2015, https://theconversation.com/the-origins -of-the-all-powerful-news-anchor-37874.

8. See, for example: https://news.gallup.com/poll/350486/record-high -support-same-sex-marriage.aspx.

9. Jonathan Haidt, "Why the Past 10 Years of American Life Have Been Uniquely Stupid," *The Atlantic*, April 11, 2022, https://www.theatlantic .com/magazine/archive/2022/05/social-media-democracy-trust-babel /629369/.

10. @tpjmd, June 4, 2022, https://twitter.com/tpjmd/status/1533188688 322101249; accessed March 2023.

CHAPTER 2: WHO NEEDS CHURCH, ANYWAY?

1. See Matthew 22:15–22; Mark 12:13–17.

2. William Shakespeare, *The Merchant of Venice*, 1.3.425.

3. Abraham Lincoln, "The Gettysburg Address," November 19, 1863.

4. Martin Luther King Jr., "I Have a Dream," The March on Washington for Jobs and Freedom, August 28, 1963.

5. Barack Obama, "Barack Obama's Race Speech at the Constitution Center," National Constitution Center, March 18, 2008, https:// constitutioncenter.org/amoreperfectunion/docs/Race_Speech _Transcript.pdf. Note: "a Constitution that had at is [*sic*] very core . . ."

6. Peggy Noonan, "Trump and the Rise of the Unprotected," *The Wall Street Journal*, February 25, 2016, https://www.wsj.com/articles/trump -and-the-rise-of-the-unprotected-1456448550.

7. Jonathan Haidt, *The Righteous Mind: Why Good People Are Divided by*

Politics and Religion (New York: Vintage Books, 2013), part 2, "There's More to Morality than Harm and Fairness."

8. William Shakespeare, *Hamlet*, 1.3.84.

CHAPTER 3: WHAT DOES IT MEAN TO BELIEVE?

1. This proposition rankles some moderns but is inescapably true. In addition to the examples presented in the body of this paragraph, the underpinnings of secular humanism—which is our era's ruling moral framework—are likewise unprovable. While we claim that the fundamental equality of all persons is intuitive, for instance, to say so is to concede that it cannot be proven or externally verified. We accept this point because we choose to accept it on its intrinsic merits, and this acceptance is a tacit admission that the scientific method cannot demonstrate all truth. If we wish to claim the scientific method is the *only* method for discovering truth, we are left with great agility in discovering how things work, but no knowledge at all about what matters and why.

   Moreover, there is undoubtedly a friction here in that I argue for the primacy of a personal spiritual experience in coming to know the veracity of universal truth-claims. I recognize this problem but believe the point stands even so. The friction is certainly not unique to our religion; engagement with *any* religion asks us to base our behavior on a personal reaction to a set of universal truth-claims. We can try to make such decisions on purely objective cognitive grounds—for instance, by attempting to work our way through our own theodicy—but my experience is that such a purely intellectual approach to matters of faith rarely supplies the substance needed to sustain meaningful faith.

2. See David A. Bednar, "Patterns of Light" (video), The Church of Jesus Christ of Latter-day Saints, 2012, https://www.churchofjesuschrist.org/media/video/2012-01-0012-patterns-of-light-spirit-of-revelation?lang=eng.

3. Remember that overwhelming evidence may be of the kind the seeker finds personally convincing. The rules here differ from those of the scientific method. Thus, one truly transcendent experience may outweigh a great deal of supposedly more objective evidence.

4. Bill N. Hansen, Lisa N. Hansen, "Nephi's Courage," *Children's Songbook*, 120.

5. Harold B. Lee, *Church News*, July 15, 1972, 4.

6. Jonathan Haidt, *The Righteous Mind: Why Good People Are Divided by Politics and Religion* (New York: Vintage Books, 2013), chapter 3.

7. See Haidt, *The Righteous Mind*.

8. Lawrence E. Corbridge, "Stand Forever," BYU Speeches, January 22, 2019, https://speeches.byu.edu/talks/lawrence-e-corbridge/stand-for-ever/.

9. Carry Cropper, "Doubting Toward Faith," BYU College of Humanities, https://humanities.byu.edu/doubting-toward-faith/.

10. Dieter F. Uchtdorf, "Come, Join with Us," *Ensign*, November 2013.

11. To be clear: note that I am *not* talking about discovering truth outside the church. I am talking here about a focus on tearing down belief for destruction's sake.

12. I should acknowledge here a difference between the sixth kind of doubt I described and neutral skepticism. We are called to be rational, to engage our hearts and our minds in the journey of discipleship, and to gain and understand our beliefs. If I am "skeptical"—and by "skeptical" I mean that I continue to be intellectually alert and to ask questions—then that is all for the good. If we wish to call the attitude that leads to such interrogation "doubt," I would classify it as closer to the first type of doubt above. What I am describing here, however, is different. This sixth kind of doubt is unchristian not because it insists on questioning but because it actually takes pleasure in tearing down belief, in deconstructing what others (or the self) have built. Just as pride gets no satisfaction in having a thing but only in having more of a thing than someone else, this type of doubt gets no satisfaction from asking or answering questions, but only in lessening believing. It could be argued that no one would really engage in this type of doubt, but my observation of modernity tells me there is an entire strain of self-satisfied "intellectualism" that does just that.

13. Dieter F. Uchtdorf, "Acting on the Truths of the Gospel of Jesus Christ" (worldwide leadership training meeting, January 2012), broadcasts.ChurchofJesusChrist.org.

CHAPTER 4: WHY AND HOW WE BELIEVE

1. Quoted in Geoff Nelson, "On 'Praying with Your Feet,'" *Dialogue: A Journal of Mormon Thought* 45, no. 4 (winter 2012), 173, https://doi.org/10.5406/dialjmormthou.45.4.0171; emphasis in original. Russell Hancock gives a much more nuanced accounting of the process; I invite you to read the essay in its entirety.

2. W. H. Auden, *Collected Poems of W. H. Auden* (New York: Vintage, 1991), 313.

3. William James, "The Will to Believe," *The New World* 5 (June 1896), 344, https://books.google.com/books?id=6OAWAQAAIAAJ&pg=PA344.

4. Terryl Givens, Fiona Givens, *The God Who Weeps: How Mormonism Makes Sense of Life* (Salt Lake City: Ensign Peak, 2012), 4.

5. "Letter to William Phelps, 27 November 1832," *Documents, Volume 2: July 1831–January 1833,* ed. Matthew C. Godfrey et al, *The Joseph Smith Papers* (Salt Lake City: Church Historian's Press, 2013), 320.

6. Bertrand Russell, "A Free Man's Worship," December 1903, https://www3.nd.edu/~afreddos/courses/264/fmw.htm.

7. Yuval Noah Harari, *Homo Deus: A Brief History of Tomorrow* (New York: Harper, 2017), 333.

8. Naomi W. Randall, "I Am a Child of God," *Hymns* (1985), no. 301.

9. Beverly Campbell made this point a number of years ago in her book *Eve and the Choice Made in Eden.* The point has recently been made forcefully by the Givenses in *The Christ Who Heals* (chapter 3 and elsewhere) and by Terryl Givens in *Wrestling the Angel* (chapter 18).

10. See Sara Konrath et al, "Changes in Dispositional Empathy in American College Students Over Time: A Meta-analysis," *Personality and Social Psychology Review* 15, no. 2 (2010), 180–98, https://doi.org/10.1177/1088868310377395.

11. While the actions of Utahns in general don't completely track with the actions of Church members, one of the most heartening articles I've read in years was a recent extended essay in the *Washington Post* regarding how Utah has both formally and informally refused to succumb to recent efforts to deny refugees entry into the United States. The

governor went so far as to send a letter to the White House stating, "Utah's unique history informs our approach to refugees. Our state was founded by religious refugees fleeing persecution in the eastern United States. Those experiences and hardships of our pioneer ancestors 170 years ago are still fresh in the mind of many Utahns. As a result, we empathize deeply with individuals and groups who have been forced from their homes and we love giving them a new home and a new life." Mackenzie Stauffer, "In Letter to Trump, Gov. Herbert Asks for More Refugees to Resettle in Utah," KJZZ.com, November 1, 2019, https://kjzz.com/news/local/in-letter-to-trump-gov-herbert-asks-for-more-refugees-to-resettle-in-utah.

12. This point is made most forcefully in Terryl and Fiona Givens's *The God Who Weeps*, but their point is one that runs consistently through Restoration scripture, perhaps most powerfully in Moses 7, but in multiple other places as references in this section and elsewhere, as well.

13. See Dallin H. Oaks, "Love and Law," *Ensign*, November 2009; "Divine Love and the Father's Plan," *Liahona*, May 2022.

14. Gerrit W. Gong, "Covenant Belonging," *Ensign*, November 2019.

15. Neal A. Maxwell, "According to the Desire of [Our] Hearts," *Ensign*, November 1996.

16. He does not list each of the influences I do here, but he does state categorically that our desires will determine our eternal destiny; the relative unimportance of the influences listed here can thus be fairly inferred.

17. Jean M. Twenge, "Have Smartphones Destroyed a Generation?" *The Atlantic*, September 2017, https://www.theatlantic.com/magazine/archive/2017/09/has-the-smartphone-destroyed-a-generation/534198/.

18. Sherry Turkle, *Alone Together: Why We Expect More from Technology and Less from Each Other* (New York: Basic Books, 2012).

19. See "America Pulls Back From Values That Once Defined It, WSJ-NORC Poll Finds," *Wall Street Journal*, https://www.wsj.com/articles/americans-pull-back-from-values-that-once-defined-u-s-wsj-norc-poll-finds-df8534cd.

20. David Brooks, *The Second Mountain: The Quest for a Moral Life* (New York: Random House, 2019), 31.

21. Robert Putnam, *Bowling Alone: The Collapse and Revival of American Community* (New York: Simon & Schuster, 2000).

22. "Penn Research Shows That Mormons Are Generous and Active in Helping Others," *Penn Today*, https://penntoday.upenn.edu/news/penn -research-shows-mormons-are-generous-and-active-helping-others.

23. There are many discussions of this trend, but for example, see: Alvin Chang, "White America Is Quietly Self-Segregating," *Vox*, July 31, 2018, https://www.vox.com/2017/1/18/14296126/white-segregated -suburb-neighborhood-cartoon.

24. Eugene England, "Why the Church Is As True As the Gospel," https:// www.eugeneengland.org/why-the-church-is-as-true-as-the-gospel; see also Eugene England, *Why The Church Is As True As the Gospel* (Salt Lake City: Bookcraft), 1986.

CHAPTER 5: THE ETHICS OF FAITH

1. Reyna I. Aburto, "Thru Cloud and Sunshine, Lord, Abide with Me!" *Ensign*, November 2019.

2. One review astutely pointed out that our religion, probably uniquely, asks its members to reaffirm our commitment to certain theological premises (about Heavenly Father, Jesus Christ, the restored gospel, and modern prophets) through the temple recommend process. It is certainly true that these requested affirmations add a unique element to our faith life. I am *not* giving advice about how to answer these questions in the face of waxing and waning spiritual confidence. Even so, I will point out that the questions are carefully worded and that, for instance, the word *know* never appears in any of them. Those that deal with beliefs ask about things like "having faith in" and "sustaining."

3. C. S. Lewis, *The Screwtape Letters* (Geoffrey Bles, 1942), chapter VIII.

4. Jeffrey R. Holland, "Cast Not Therefore Away Thy Confidence," BYU Speeches, March 2, 1999, https://speeches.byu.edu/talks/jeffrey-r -holland/cast-not-away-therefore-your-confidence/.

5. See Dallin H. Oaks, "The Challenge to Become," *Ensign*, November 2000.

6. See Neal A. Maxwell, "Content with the Things Allotted unto Us,"

Ensign, May 2000. See also Neal A. Maxwell, "According to the Desires of [Our] Hearts," *Ensign*, November 1996.

7. See Jeffrey R. Holland, "Behold Thy Mother," *Ensign*, November 2015. Elder Holland said: "And, I should mention, this son's sexual orientation did not somehow miraculously change—no one expected it would."

8. Elder Dale G. Renlund outlined a similar analogy—but with different emphasis—in his first general conference talk as an Apostle. See Dale G. Renlund, "Preserving the Heart's Mighty Change," *Ensign*, November 2009.

9. *Lectures on Faith* famously teaches that "faith" is a "principle of action." I am not arguing against that here. Indeed, that is precisely my point: "faith" is the principle that moves us to act despite the rise and fall of our believing.

10. William Shakespeare, *Hamlet*, 1.3.84.

11. Josiah Royce, *The Philosophy of Loyalty* (New York: The Macmillan Company, 1914), 42.

12. Daniel Trotta, "Letters reveal Mother Teresa's doubt about faith," Reuters, August 24, 2007, https://www.reuters.com/article/us-teresa -letters/letters-reveal-mother-teresas-doubt-about-faith-idUSN243550 6020070824.

13. C. S. Lewis, *A Grief Observed* (San Francisco: Harper, 1961), 6.

14. Jeffrey R. Holland, "None Were with Him," *Ensign*, May 2009.

15. Jeffrey R. Holland, "The Hands of the Fathers," *Ensign*, May 1999.

16. Jeffrey R. Holland, "Behold Thy Mother," *Ensign*, November 2015.

CHAPTER 6: WHEN BELIEF FADES

1. "Women as Witnesses," in Catherine Clark Kroeger and Mary J. Evans, eds., *The IVP Women's Bible Commentary* (Downers Grove, IL: Intervarsity Press, 2002), 560–61.

2. See 1 Corinthians 15:1–11.

3. *Women in Scripture: A Dictionary of Named and Unnamed Women in the Hebrew Bible, the Apocryphal/Deuterocanonical Books, and the New Testament* (Boston: Houghton Mifflin, 2000), 120–23.

4. "Gospel of John," in Carol A. Newsom, Sharon H. Ringe, and Jacqueline E. Lapsley, eds., *Women's Bible Commentary: 20th Anniversary Edition* (Louisville: Westminster John Knox Press, 1992, 2012) 527–29.

5. Although, as mentioned, the accuracy of that interpretation is debatable, given the sparse and sometimes apparently conflicting details in the various accounts.

6. Alma 40:23.

7. See Matthew 26:69–75; Mark 14:66–72; Luke 22:54–62; John 18:15–27.

8. Psalm 30:5.

9. Rosemary M. Wixom, "Returning to Faith," *Ensign*, May 2015.

10. Hilaire Belloc, "The Prophet Lost in the Hills at Evening," https://www.gutenberg.org/files/60487/60487-h/60487-h.htm.

11. See Emma Lou Warner Thayne, *The Place of Knowing: A Spiritual Autobiography* (iUniverse, 2011). I should note here that the accident later came to take on spiritual overtones that eventually outweighed its immediate, catastrophic impact. Through a complex and subtle process of spiritual self-discovery, she eventually decided that she actually briefly died after the collision, and then visited heaven and was sent back to earth to preach of heaven's love and beauty. I'm frankly not much for "I've come back from heaven with a message" narratives, but this book is striking for its candor, kindness, poetry, and beauty, and the spiritual overtones that the accident's aftermath eventually acquires do nothing to change its initial horror.

12. Ether 12:41.

13. John 1:46.

CHAPTER 7: A CHURCH BOTH LIVING AND TRUE

1. Margaret Blair Young, "To The Pastor," https://bycommonconsent.com/2007/05/03/to-the-pastor/.

2. Bruce C. and Marie K. Hafen's recent book *Faith Is Not Blind* (Deseret Book, 2018) speaks about a gap in a somewhat similar context, though we take different approaches on the subject.

3. It's fair to note that many modern churches don't spend a lot of time

or energy attempting to demonstrate that they directly reflect "the same organization that existed in the Primitive Church" (Articles of Faith 1:6)—which is another way we are a fairly "peculiar people" (Deuteronomy 14:2; 26:18; Titus 2:14; 1 Peter 2:9). Even so, it is true that the thrust of the Protestant project was to attempt to better align the then-modern church with Christ's teachings. As most modern churches descend from either Catholicism or Protestantism, it seems fair to say that they have attempted to reflect at least the intent—if not the form and organization—of the early Church.

4. Dieter F. Uchtdorf, "Are You Sleeping through the Restoration?" *Ensign*, May 2014.

5. "LDS Church changes temple ceremony; faithful feminists will see revisions and additions as a 'leap forward,'" *Salt Lake Tribune*, Jan. 2, 2019, https://www.sltrib.com/religion/2019/01/02/lds-church -releases/.

6. See Edward Kimball, *Spencer W. Kimball: A Biography* (Salt Lake City: Bookcraft, 1977).

7. See Edward Kimball, *Lengthen Your Stride: The Presidency of Spencer W. Kimball* (Salt Lake City: Deseret Book, 2005).

8. See Edward Kimball, *Spencer W. Kimball*, 194.

9. The evidence concerning the exact contours of Joseph Smith's polygamous marriages is complicated and beyond the scope of this work. Many scholars have noted that whatever the introduction of polygamy was, it does *not* seem to have been a mere sham to allow Joseph to exercise his sexual appetites. This all is discussed in the Church's Gospel Topics essays on plural marriage. In addition, Brain C. and Laura H. Hales's book *Joseph Smith's Polygamy: Toward a Better Understanding* contains a wealth of information.

10. Though Joseph Smith was also limited by the cultural milieu in which he came of age and said, wrote, and did things that would be offensive by modern sensibilities, he seems to have consistently preached a racially inclusive gospel, and there is no convincing evidence that the priesthood or temple bans started with him. See also Paul Reeve's *Religion of a Different Color: Race and the Mormon Struggle for Whiteness* (Oxford University Press, 2015).

11. Russell M. Nelson, "Let God Prevail," *Ensign*, November 2020.
12. Dallin H. Oaks, "Racism and Other Challenges" (Brigham Young University devotional, October 27, 2020), speeches.byu.edu.
13. M. Russell Ballard, "Questions and Answers," BYU Speeches, November 14, 2017, https://speeches.byu.edu/talks/m-russell-ballard/questions-and-answers/.
14. Dieter F. Uchtdorf, "Come, Join with Us," *Ensign*, November 2013.
15. Jeffrey R. Holland, "Lord, I Believe," *Ensign*, May 2013.
16. Neal A. Maxwell, "Jesus of Nazareth, Savior and King," *Ensign*, May 1976.
17. Eugene England, "Why the Church Is As True As the Gospel," https://www.eugeneengland.org/why-the-church-is-as-true-as-the-gospel; see also Eugene England, *Why The Church Is As True As the Gospel* (Salt Lake City: Bookcraft), 1986.

CHAPTER 8: HEALING THE BODY OF CHRIST

1. See Google Books Ngram Viewer, "marginalized," https://books.google.com/ngrams/graph?content=marginalized&year_start=1800&year_end=2019&corpus=26&smoothing=0.
2. Rachel Sterzer Gibson, "How to make Relief Society a safe place for every sister, the general presidency emphasizes at BYU Women's Conference," *Church News*, April 29, 2021, https://www.thechurchnews.com/2021/4/29/23217229/byu-womens-conference-relief-society-a-safe-place-belonging.
3. CarrieAnne Simonini DeLoach, in Melissa Wei-Tsing Inouye and Kate Holbrook, eds., *Every Needful Thing: Essays on the Life of the Mind and Heart* (BYU Maxwell Institute/Deseret Book, 2023), 134–35.
4. Neal A. Maxwell, "Content with the Things Allotted unto Us," *Ensign*, May 2000.
5. I've made this argument at more length in the essay "Empathy and the Atonement," *BYU Studies Quarterly* 55, no. 4.
6. I should note that in the years since 2020, we *have* heard "talk after talk" about just this thing, both in general conference and in other forums.

NOTES

7. In Trent Toone, "Brother Ahmad S. Corbitt: How activism against the Church can blind, mislead 'valiant' souls," *Church News*, November 1, 2022, https://www.thechurchnews.com/leaders/2022/11/1/23424931/brother-ahmad-s-corbitt-activism-discipleship.

8. Russell M. Nelson, "The Love and Laws of God," BYU Speeches, September 17, 2019, https://speeches.byu.edu/talks/russell-m-nelson/love-laws-god/.

9. Letter from Spencer W. Kimball to Edward L. Kimball, March 11, 1963. See Edward L. Kimball, "Spencer W. Kimball and the Revelation on Priesthood," *BYU Studies Quarterly* 47, no. 2 (2008), 4, https://byustudies.byu.edu/article/spencer-w-kimball-and-the-revelation-on-priesthood/.

10. Russell M. Nelson (@NelsonRussellM), Twitter, June 1, 2020, https://twitter.com/NelsonRussellM/status/1267575018642276352.

11. Déborah Aléxis, "Déborah Aléxis: BYU must act to make black students feel safe and welcome," *The Salt Lake Tribune*, June 17, 2020, https://www.sltrib.com/opinion/commentary/2020/06/17/dborah-alxis-byu-must-act/.

12. "Report and Recommendations of the BYU Committee on Race, Equity, and Belonging," February 25, 2021, https://race.byu.edu/00000177-d543-dfa9-a7ff-d5cfc1dc0000/race-equity-belonging-report-feb-25-2021.

13. Ryan Gabriel, "Healing Racism through Jesus Christ" (Brigham Young University devotional, April 6, 2021), speeches.byu.edu.

14. Bob Rees, "Robert A. Rees: What happens to a dream deferred?" *The Salt Lake Tribune*, July 6, 2020, https://www.sltrib.com/opinion/commentary/2020/07/06/robert-rees-what-happens/.

15. See Darius Gray, "A 54-Year Journey Toward Racial Equality in the Mormon Church," University of Utah, June 29, 2018, https://unews.utah.edu/university-of-utah-examines-race-in-the-lds-church-since-1978-revelation/, https://youtu.be/QWjFf3qV2pk.

NOTES

CHAPTER 9: BELIEVING AND BECOMING

1. See "Wave—particle duality," Wikipedia, https://en.wikipedia.org /wiki/Wave-particle_duality.
2. Eliza R. Snow, "My Father in Heaven," Oct. 1845, *Times and Seasons* (Nauvoo, IL), Nov. 15, 1845, vol. 6, no. 17.
3. See Morgan Jacobsen, "Noted LDS poet, author Emma Lou Thayne dies at 90," *Deseret News*, December 6, 2014, https://www.deseret .com/2014/12/6/20554287/noted-lds-poet-author-emma-lou-thayne -dies-at-90.
4. Of course I claim no real ability to judge who has been sanctified, but I will take Elder Jeffrey R. Holland's remark at Emma Lou's funeral that she had lived a "perfect Mormon life" as implicit endorsement.
5. "A Message from the First Presidency," The Church of Jesus Christ of Latter-day Saints, January 16, 2018, https://www.churchofjesuschrist .org/bc/content/ldsorg/church/news/2018/01/19/2018-01-1000-a -message-from-the-first-presidency.pdf?lang=eng.
6. See Dallin H. Oaks, "The Challenge to Become," *Ensign*, November 2000.
7. Russell M. Nelson, "Overcome the World and Find Rest," *Liahona*, November 2022.
8. For example, see: David A. Bednar, "Prepared to Obtain Every Needful Thing," Ensign, May 2019.
9. Gerrit W. Gong, "Covenant Belonging," *Ensign*, November 2019.
10. Russell M. Nelson, "Let God Prevail," *Ensign*, November 2020.
11. Gilbert K. Chesterton, *Orthodoxy* (1908), chapter 2.
12. James Montgomery, "A Poor Wayfaring Man of Grief," *Hymns* (1985), no. 29.

AFTERWORD: HEARING THE MUSIC AGAIN

1. Wilford W. Andersen, "The Music of the Gospel," *Ensign*, May 2015.
2. Emma Lou Warner Thayne, *The Place of Knowing* (Bloomington, Ind.: iUniverse, 2011), 45–46.
3. In Marianne Holman Prescott, "Elder Holland shares lessons he

learned from Elder Maxwell, calls for 'Mormon studies' name change," *Church News*, November 14, 2018, https://www.thechurchnews .com/2018/11/14/23264505/elder-holland-shares-lessons-he-learned -from-elder-maxwell-calls-for-mormon-studies-name-change.